HOT TOPICS

RACISM IN AMERICA

A LONG HISTORY OF HATE

By Meghan Green

Portions of this book originally appeared in *Racism* by David Robson.

Published in 2018 by
Lucent Press, an Imprint of Greenhaven Publishing, LLC
353 3rd Avenue
Suite 255
New York, NY 10010

Designer: Seth Hughes
Editor: Jennifer Lombardo

Cataloging-in-Publication Data

Names: Green, Meghan.
Title: Racism in America: a long history of hate / Meghan Green.
Description: New York : Lucent Press, 2018. | Series: Hot topics | Includes index.
Identifiers: ISBN 9781534561434 (library bound) | ISBN 9781534561441 (ebook)
Subjects: LCSH: Racism–United States–Juvenile literature. | United States–Race relations--Juvenile literature. | Race discrimination–United States–Juvenile literature.
Classification: LCC E184.A1 G74 2018 | DDC 305.800973–dc23

Printed in the United States of America

CPSIA compliance information: Batch #BS17KL: For further information contact Greenhaven Publishing LLC, New York, New York at 1-844-317-7404.

Please visit our website, www.greenhavenpublishing.com. For a free color catalog of all our high-quality books, call toll free 1-844-317-7404 or fax 1-844-317-7405.

CONTENTS

FOREWORD

Adolescence is a time when many people begin to take notice of the world around them. News channels, blogs, and talk radio shows are constantly promoting one view or another; very few are unbiased. Young people also hear conflicting information from parents, friends, teachers, and acquaintances. Often, they will hear only one side of an issue or be given flawed information. People who are trying to support a particular viewpoint may cite inaccurate facts and statistics on their blogs, and news programs present many conflicting views of important issues in our society. In a world where it seems everyone has a platform to share their thoughts, it can be difficult to find unbiased, accurate information about important issues.

It is not only facts that are important. In blog posts, in comments on online videos, and on talk shows, people will share opinions that are not necessarily true or false, but can still have a strong impact. For example, many young people struggle with their body image. Seeing or hearing negative comments about particular body types online can have a huge effect on the way someone views himself or herself and may lead to depression and anxiety. Although it is important not to keep information hidden from young people under the guise of protecting them, it is equally important to offer encouragement on issues that affect their mental health.

The titles in the Hot Topics series provide readers with different viewpoints on important issues in today's society. Many of these issues, such as teen pregnancy and Internet safety, are of immediate concern to young people. This series aims to give readers factual context on these crucial topics in a way that lets them form their own opinions. The facts presented throughout also serve to empower readers to help themselves or support people they know who are struggling with many of the challenges adolescents face today. Although negative viewpoints are not ignored or downplayed, this series allows young people to see that the challenges they face are not insurmountable. Eating disorders can be overcome, the Internet can be navigated safely, and pregnant teens do not have to feel hopeless.

Quotes encompassing all viewpoints are presented and cited so readers can trace them back to their original source, verifying for themselves whether the information comes from a reputable place. Additional books and websites are listed, giving readers a starting point from which to continue their own research. Chapter questions encourage discussion, allowing young people to hear and understand their classmates' points of view as they further solidify their own. Full-color photographs and enlightening charts provide a deeper understanding of the topics at hand. All of these features augment the informative text, helping young people understand the world they live in and formulate their own opinions concerning the best way they can improve it.

INTRODUCTION

Racism Is Not New

Throughout world history, certain groups have proclaimed that lighter skin is better than darker skin. White Europeans, most notably the Vikings, the Romans, and the British, spread across the globe in search of money and power. The impact of these groups can still be seen in some countries today.

The United States was founded as a group of British colonies by white people trying to escape religious persecution in England, but the British were not the only people who lived there. Before the 1800s, the Spanish, French, and Dutch all claimed portions of what is now the United States. Each of these groups persecuted the Native Americans who were already living there when the settlers arrived; the British and Europeans took Native American lands, broke treaties, and attempted to exterminate various Native American groups.

After the United States became an independent country, this persecution persisted and affected national policy. Most notably, in the 1830s, Andrew Jackson signed legislation that eventually forced the Cherokee people to move from present-day Georgia, Tennessee, Alabama, North Carolina, and Florida to present-day Oklahoma so white people could settle and plant crops where the Cherokee had once lived. This journey was often difficult and dangerous, and many people died on the way, which led to this event being called the Trail of Tears. Today, negative attitudes regarding Native Americans and their lands still exist.

The Trail of Tears is one of the most obvious examples of racism against Native Americans, but more subtle racism still exists today.

Black people have also had an especially difficult time in the United States from the beginning of the nation's history. In 1619, the first slaves were brought from Africa to the colony of Virginia. Slavery became a national institution and was responsible for much of the economic growth in the United States. Although slavery was eventually abolished, racist attitudes against black people persist throughout the country.

As time went on and people from other countries began immigrating to the United States, they, too, often faced racism when they arrived. Although people of typically white nationalities, such as the Irish and Italians, were discriminated against, this was not due to the color of their skin, and they were eventually societally accepted in the United States. However, for Arabs, Middle Easterners, Latinx, East Asians, and Southeast Asians, their skin color has made them easy targets for discrimination and sometimes violence.

Racism Still Exists

When President Barack Obama was elected in 2008, many people took this as proof that racism no longer existed in the United States. However, despite the feelings of hope surrounding Obama's historic election and the excitement over his Nobel Peace Prize, racism still exists in the United States and around the world. For example, Obama received unprecedented Secret Service security protection long before Election Day. No candidate for president had received protection so early on the campaign trail before. In the early days of Obama's campaign, Secret Service agents, charged with guarding the president and presidential candidates, investigated death threats, many of which mentioned his race, on an almost daily basis. After Obama's inauguration in January 2009, death threats against him soared, with the Secret Service fielding at least 30 each day. The overwhelming number of threats—much higher than those against any other president—stretched the Secret Service to the breaking

The Black Lives Matter movement has drawn attention to the continuing issue of racism in the United States.

point, as agents often worked longer hours to handle the increased workload.

The emergence of the Black Lives Matter (BLM) movement in 2013 was in response to the racism that black people still experience in America today. However, even after seeing multiple news stories and videos in which unarmed black people were the victims of police brutality, a number of people still denied that racism exists. Some people have difficulty recognizing systemic, or institutional, racism, which is racism that is "structured into political and social institutions. It occurs when [organizations], institutions or governments discriminate, either deliberately or indirectly, against certain groups of people to limit their rights."[1]

One of the most glaring examples of systemic racism in America today is the number of young black and Hispanic men in prison compared to the number of white men. Although only about 14 percent of drug users are black, 45 percent of people arrested for drug charges are black. These statistics point out a vast difference in the way black and white people are treated by the judicial system, as two African American scholars explained:

> *Although no longer inscribed in law, [racism] is implicit to processes of law enforcement, prosecution, and incarceration, guiding the behavior of police, prosecutors, judges, juries, wardens, and parole boards. Hence, African Americans continue to experience higher rates of incarceration than do whites charged with similar crimes, endure longer sentences for the same classes of crimes perpetrated by whites, and, compared to white inmates, receive far less consideration by parole boards when being considered for release.*[2]

Although racism against black people in particular is often in the news, this is not the only group that is discriminated against. During Donald Trump's presidential campaign, he verbally attacked undocumented Mexican immigrants, saying that many who came to the United States were criminals. This accusation frightened many Americans who then supported Trump's goal to build a wall along the United States–Mexico border. After Trump was elected, the number of crimes against people who did not appear to be white rose dramatically.

Other groups, such as Native American and Asian American people, are often ignored by the media, but this does not mean they do not experience racism. It means the racism is hidden, which makes it harder to fight.

Although some people continue to deny it, racism is unfortunately still widespread in the United States and throughout the world. Learning about racism and the distressing effects it has on its victims is the first step toward ending it.

CHAPTER 1

Modern-Day Racism

Racism is the belief that one race is better than another. Racism involves prejudice, or negative opinions, judgments, and attitudes about people based on their race. David T. Wellman, author of *Portraits of White Racism*, explained that racism is more than just bias against a group of people based on skin color. Wellman defined racism as a "system of advantage based on race."[3] In other words, racism involves not only discriminating against one race but also upholding the advantages another race enjoys, including better opportunities for education, housing, and employment.

In the past, people were often more openly racist. Advertisements that used racial stereotypes to sell products were common, as were racial slurs, which are insulting nicknames for people of a certain race. After the civil rights movement of the 1960s, attitudes regarding racism slowly began to change. Unfortunately, racism did not disappear; it simply became less acceptable to speak about openly. In modern society, openly racist acts are often viewed by the general population as shocking, while subtly racist acts often go unnoticed or even defended by those who are not victims.

Hate Crimes in the United States

Racism can be expressed in violent ways. Acts of violence or vandalism against a person because of his or her race, ethnicity, religion, or sexual orientation are called hate crimes, and thousands of people are victims each year. In the United States, 5,479 hate crimes were reported in 2015, a small decrease from 2013, when 5,928 hate crimes were reported. Police determined that 11 percent of these hate crimes were racially motivated. The day after Donald Trump was elected president in 2016, the number of reported hate crimes rose dramatically, with 202 incidents reported on November 9

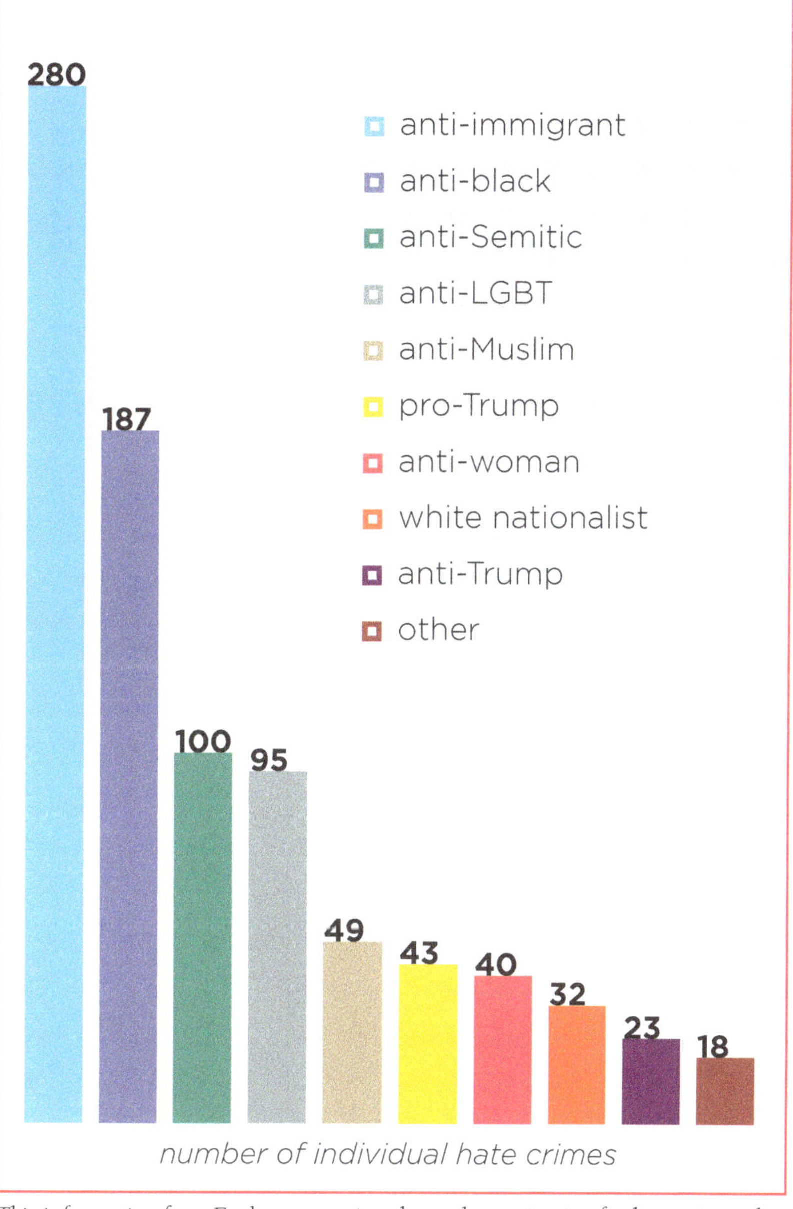

This information from Forbes *magazine shows the motivation for hate crimes that happened in November 2016.*

alone. According to *Forbes* magazine, "Many of those incidents involved harassers invoking Trump's name, making it clear that the outbreak of hate was primarily due to his success in the election."[4]

Non-white immigrants, black people, and Jewish people are primary targets for hate crimes. Anti-immigrant sentiments increased during Trump's election campaign as he blamed Mexican and Muslim people for many of America's safety concerns. When people speak negatively about immigrants, they generally mean immigrants who are not white. Although white people who come from Europe to live in the United States are also immigrants, there is little, if any, negative feeling toward them from the general population. According to a poll by Morning Consult, a neutral media and technology company, many Americans favor immigrants from Europe and Asia over immigrants from other continents.

In some cases, hate crimes are not crimes committed by one person acting alone. Some perpetrators identify themselves as members of an organized group. The Southern Poverty Law Center (SPLC), a nonprofit social justice group, identified 892 active hate groups in the United States in 2015, up from 784 the previous year. Although not all of these groups are known to be violent, sociologists argue that their existence alone can spark acts of racist violence.

Racism in Other Countries

Although thousands of racially motivated crimes are committed in the United States each year, other countries are not immune to the phenomenon. Finland, England, Ireland, China, Greece, Sweden, Denmark, Germany, Spain, and France are but a few of the countries where this kind of violence has risen. In June 2016, the United Kingdom (UK)—England, Northern Ireland, Wales, and Scotland—voted to leave the European Union (EU). This became known as Brexit, a combination of the words "Britain" and "exit." One major motivation for those who voted to leave was to make it harder for immigrants to enter the country. As with Trump's election, after Brexit, the number of hate crimes rose dramatically. British police reported a 57 percent increase in hate crimes in the four days after the Brexit vote. However, unlike in the United States, even white immigrants are often targeted in the UK.

In Europe and South America particularly, fans of soccer, which is called football in many other countries, regularly show their racist tendencies. Amid the cheers and boos typical of any sporting event, extreme fans known as hooligans frequently shout racial insults, throw garbage, and make monkey noises at black players—insinuating that people of color resemble monkeys. "I think it's unacceptable to behave like that in a football stadium but also in any other walk of life," said María Jesús San Segundo, Spain's education and science minister from 2004 to 2006. "It shows a lack of education … Young people have to realise that regardless of sex, colour or culture every human being is the same."[5]

Many fans consider the behavior little more than a show of enthusiasm for their own team. "The kids' chanting last night was stupid but harmless," said Alejandro, a Spanish football fan, after one such event. "Football is always about insulting the other team. The racism wasn't meant seriously."[6]

Alejandro's opinion was echoed by his friend, Miguel, who said, "We Spaniards aren't more racist than any other country. Italy has problems with football and racism, doesn't it? It's much worse than here."[7]

Italy has a population of 60 million people. However, millions of immigrants reside there illegally. Italy depends on undocumented immigrants, who are mostly from West Africa, to work long hours for little pay picking fruit, a job many Italians consider beneath them. In January 2010, some of the country's worst race riots in years erupted after two African immigrants were wounded with a pellet gun in the southern region of Calabria. Other African immigrants, who blamed racism for the attack, took to the streets in protest, throwing rocks, setting cars on fire, and clashing with local police. More than 50 immigrants and police officers were wounded in the 2 days of rioting that engulfed the entire city of Rosarno.

The incident revealed the ugly reality of Italy's dependence on cheap labor and the racism that is often involved. "This event pulled the lid off something that we who work in the sector know well but no one talks about: That many Italian economic realities are based on the exploitation of low-cost foreign labor, living in subhuman conditions, without human rights,"[8] said Flavio di Giacomo, spokesperson for the International Organization for Migration.

Discrimination at Work

Racism is not always expressed through violent actions. Racial discrimination, although typically illegal, remains common in many countries, and the United States is no exception. In 2015 alone, 31,027 cases of racial discrimination in the workplace were filed with the U.S. Equal Employment Opportunity Commission (EEOC), which is responsible for enforcing federal laws against discrimination.

Racial discrimination occurs in the workplace when a person is prevented from holding a certain job or from advancing in their career because of their race. Discriminatory practices in the workplace are reflected in the income disparity, or difference, between people of color (sometimes abbreviated as POC) and white people in the United States. According to data from the U.S. Census Bureau, black families earn on average about $40,000 per year and Hispanic families earn about $50,000, compared with white families, who earn on average $68,000. Other racial groups were not included in the study.

Although companies often try to be diverse, people of color rarely fill leadership roles in the United States. As of 2017, there are only 5 black chief executive officers (CEOs) in America's 500 biggest companies. David A. Thomas, a professor at Harvard Business School, said, "People of color who start at the same time as an equivalent white person have less of a chance of being at the top echelon [level] in 20 years, in whatever field you're talking about."[9]

Whether these employment trends will continue in the future is difficult to gauge, but without people of color in positions of leadership, many see a bleak future in which racism and oppression will surely persist. "The biggest challenge is really not having the role models, not seeing yourself, at the senior

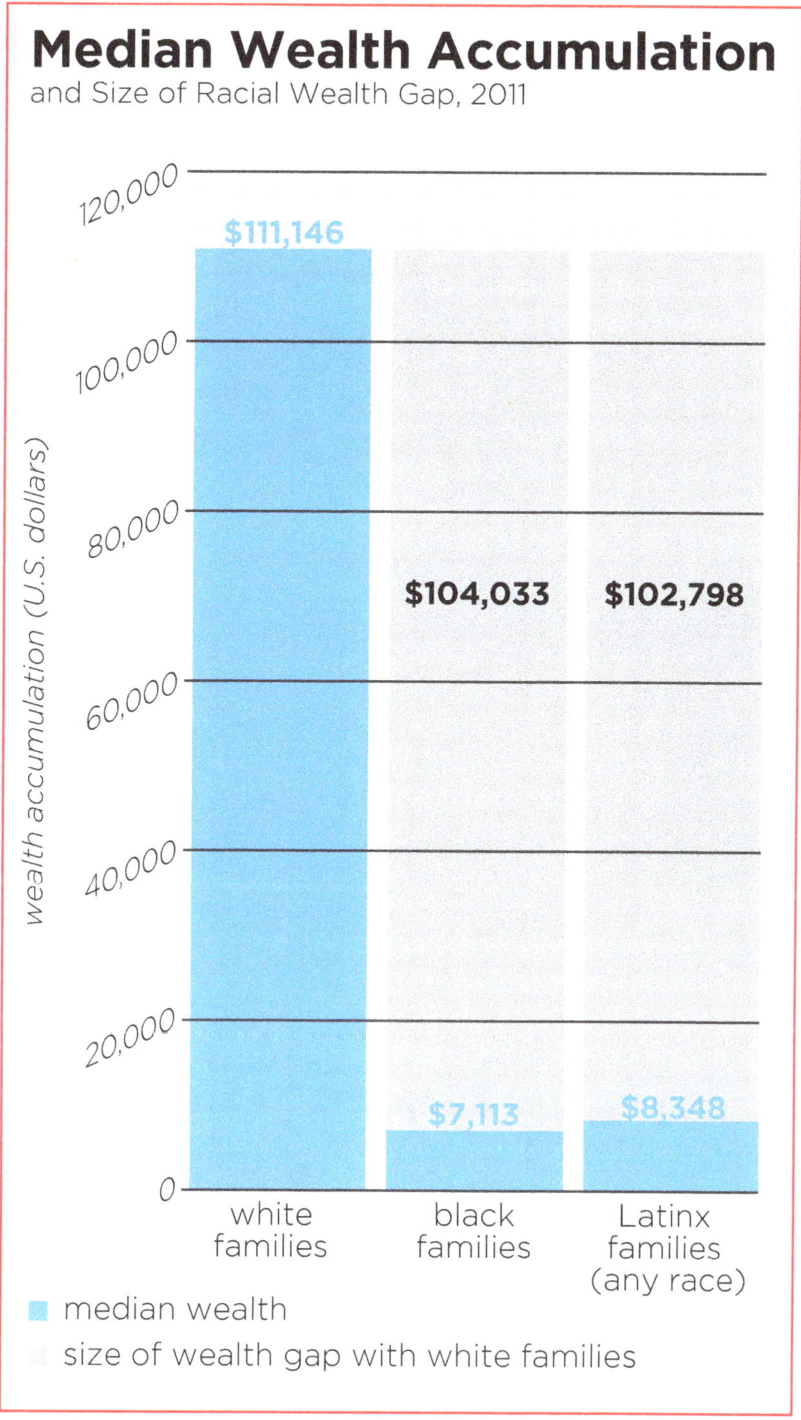

White families have significantly more wealth (savings, stock shares, investments, etc.) than families of color, as this information from Forbes *shows.*

levels early in your career,"[10] said Clarence Otis Jr., former CEO of Darden Restaurants.

Racial discrimination also occurs early in the employment process, as a 2003 study showed. Researchers Marianne Bertrand of the University of Chicago and Dean Karlan of Yale University sent out nearly 5,000 fictional résumés in Boston, Massachusetts, and Chicago, Illinois. Their résumés included some with "white-sounding" names, such as Emily and Greg, and some with "black-sounding" names, such as Lakisha and Jamal. Bertrand and Karlan discovered that the résumés with white-sounding names received 50 percent more calls for interviews than those with black-sounding names, indicating a racial prejudice in hiring practices.

People of color who do get hired may be subjected to unfair practices in the workplace. One example of this can be found in the class action lawsuit against New York City's Parks and Recreation Department. For years, people of color who worked in the department rarely received pay raises comparable with their white counterparts and were typically turned down for promotions. Banding together, the employees sued the city, and after nine years, they won their court battle. The 2008 settlement awarded the workers $21 million, much of it in back pay, and the department agreed to change its policies and procedures to ensure fairness in the future. According to the plaintiffs' attorney, Cynthia Rolling, "this case and this settlement should provide inspiration to all employees subjected to unfair and discriminatory treatment on their jobs."[11]

Racism in Education

The workplace is only one area in which racism and prejudice frequently appear. In schools, especially, various forms of racism and racial insensitivity challenge teachers and students around the world on a regular basis. For example, during Trump's presidential campaign and election, instances were reported of students chanting "build a wall" at non-white students. The news network CNN posted a video of one such incident as well as people's reactions to it on its website.

Race also plays a part in which students are able to advance to higher education. In 2014, the Pew Research Center reported that 14 percent of Hispanic students and 8 percent of black students had dropped out of high school the previous year, compared to 5 percent of white students and 4 percent of Asian students. While these numbers are at a historic low, they still represent a significant number of young adults who will have limited career choices in the future. For Native American high schoolers, the graduation rate is only 67 percent, compared to a national average of 80 percent, according to *U.S. News & World Report*. Sociologists do not believe that racism is the sole cause for this lack of achievement, but it may be one key factor, especially because race has been shown to affect other factors, such as poverty rates. In cities and on reservations, crumbling buildings, outdated textbooks, and unqualified staff discourage

Many people of color overcome the challenges stacked against them to earn their college degree, but they continue to face more challenges than their white counterparts after graduation.

students from staying in school. Each year, broken schools and financial pressures force thousands of students into the workforce before completing their high school education.

Even those who do graduate and attend college face problems. *The Atlantic* reported that black people with a college degree still face unemployment at greater rates than white people. Their unemployment rate is almost equal to white people who have only a high school degree. Black college graduates also have twice as many student loans as white college graduates, so they start off at an economic disadvantage.

RACISM AGAINST OBAMA

"I think an overwhelming portion of the intensely demonstrated animosity toward President Barack Obama is based on the fact that he is a black man, that he's African American."—Jimmy Carter, 39th president of the United States.

Quoted in Ewen MacAskill, "Jimmy Carter: Animosity Towards Barack Obama Is Due to Racism," *Guardian*, September 16, 2009.

Everyday Racism

Racism exists in many forms. Sometimes it is obvious, as with racially motivated hate crimes, and sometimes it is subtle, such as a racially insensitive comment. However, regardless of the form racism takes, it is always damaging. Racist comments, even accidental ones, give the impression that people of color are somehow inferior to whites.

Many people say or do things to people of color that are considered offensive simply because they do not consider how their actions will make the other person will feel. Other times, people are intentionally offensive. One type of racist comment is called a microaggression. Microaggressions are "brief and commonplace daily verbal, behavioral, or environmental indignities, whether intentional or unintentional, that communicate hostile, derogatory, or negative racial slights and insults toward people of color."[12] These comments are often different for different races.

For Native Americans, it may be questions such as, "Do you live in a tipi?," or the assumption that they abuse alcohol. For East Asians, it may be remarks such as, "Where are you from?," which assumes that the person was born in Asia, when in fact, many people of Asian descent are born and raised in the country they currently live in. Many people also do not take the time to find out which Asian country a person is from and tend to assume that all Asian people are Chinese. Black people may face comments such as, "You're pretty for a black girl," "You don't act like a regular black person," or "You're very well-spoken," which assumes that there is one particular type of black person and that anyone who breaks this mold is unusual. They may also have to answer questions that are differently worded than questions that are asked of white people. For instance, while a white woman may be asked, "Do you have any kids?," a black woman may be asked, "How many kids do you have?"

Arab and Middle Eastern people may be asked if they are Muslim or terrorists. Latinx people may receive comments about how they must love tacos, and many tend to assume all Latinx are Mexican. People of mixed races who appear white may be told that they are not actually people of color. Anyone who does not appear white may be complimented on their English, which assumes that they were not raised in an English-speaking country.

These are only a few of the numerous microaggressions people of all races might hear on a daily basis. Some can be directed at any race, while others are specific to one race. People who commit microaggressions often do not do so on purpose and may not see anything wrong with what they said. However, when microaggressions are experienced on a daily basis, they can be damaging, giving people of color the impression that they are outsiders in their own country. It may not seem like a big deal to ask a Latinx person if they like tacos or a black person if they like fried chicken, but these microaggressions assume that food preferences are based on genetics and disregard the fact that many people enjoy these foods regardless of skin color.

Sometimes people say things without thinking or make a genuine mistake that comes off as racist. In that case, it is extremely important for the person who made the comment to respect the other person's feelings if they are upset by the remark. If a person of color tells a white person, "That remark was racist

People of color experience microaggressions on a daily basis.

and I feel offended," the white person should not try to explain themselves by saying things such as, "It was a joke," "Here's why I said that," or "You're too sensitive." Instead, they should recognize that they accidentally hurt someone's feelings and say, "I'm sorry, I didn't realize. I'll remember that in the future."

The Myth of Reverse Racism

When white people are insulted by someone of color or excluded from certain things that are POC-specific, they sometimes say that they have experienced reverse racism, or racism against white people by people of color. They may cite the fact that there is a Black History Month but no White History Month or claim that the BLM movement spreads the idea that white people's lives do not matter. If they are called a racial slur by a person of color, they may also say they have experienced reverse racism. However, reverse racism does not exist.

Prejudice is a dislike of a person or group based on the idea that all members of that group have the same characteristics; for instance, a black person who assumes that all white people are snobby has a prejudice against white people. However, racism is a social system that disadvantages people of any non-white race. White people "do not face housing or job discrimination, police brutality, poverty, or incarceration [jail time] at the level that [people of color] do. That is not to say that they do not experience things like poverty and police brutality at all. But again, *not on the same scale*—not even close. *That* is the reality of racism."[1] Since white people will always have more privilege in places such as the United States and Europe, they still benefit from the social system even if they experience prejudice from a person of color. This is why Black History Month and BLM are not racist: Society assumes by default that white lives matter and that every month is White History Month.

1. Zeba Blay, "4 'Reverse Racism' Myths That Need to Stop," *Huffington Post*, August 26, 2015. www.huffingtonpost.com/entry/reverse-racism-isnt-a-thing_us_55d60a91e4b07addcb45da97.

The information on the next page from the Center on Juvenile and Criminal Justice shows that black, Native American, and Latinx people are far more likely to be killed by police than white people.

Groups Most Likely to Be Killed by Law Enforcement

- African Americans ages 20–24
- Native Americans ages 25–34
- Native Americans ages 35–44
- African Americans ages 25–34
- Native Americans ages 20–24
- Latinx ages 20–24
- Latinx ages 25–34
- African Americans ages 35–44
- African Americans ages 15–19
- average, all races and ages

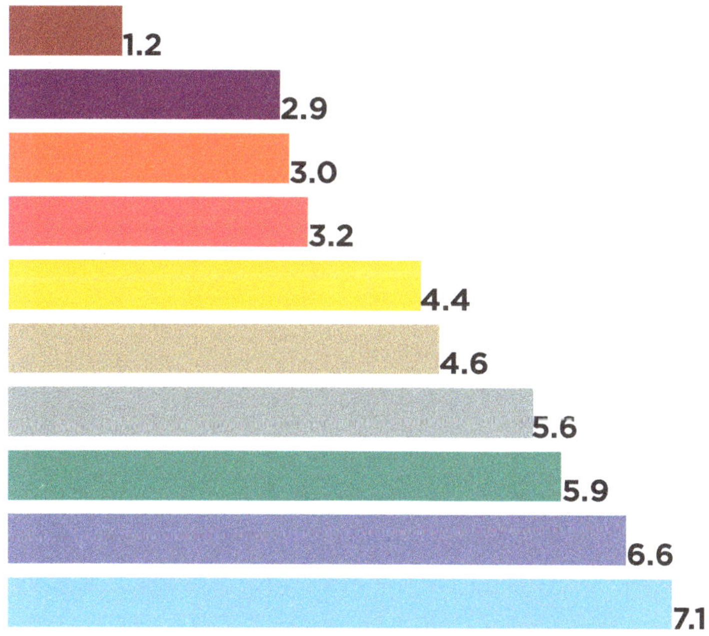

rate of law enforcement killings, per million population per year, 1999–2011

RACIAL PROFILING DOES NOT WORK

"Focusing first and foremost, or worse, solely upon such characteristics … as race, ethnicity, national origin or religion in deciding whom to investigate, arrest, and prosecute … diverts attention from actual criminal behavior and from the actual perpetrator of a crime."
–Timothy K. Lewis, former federal judge.

Quoted in Jim Lobe, "Racial Profiling Both Wrong and Counter-Productive, Says Amnesty," CommonDreams.org, September 14, 2004.

Check Your Privilege

Sometimes racism can be so subtle that a person may not even be aware of his or her own prejudices. Yet in most spheres of American life, race remains a powerful, if often unspoken, fact of life.

A 2009 study of racial attitudes in the United States found that even those people who view themselves as non-racist and tolerant may hold unconscious racial prejudices. Researchers divided 120 non-black participants into two groups: "experiencers" and "forecasters." The "experiencers" were placed in a room with a white person and a black person, both part of the study team. A prearranged scenario was played out in which the black person bumped the white person's knee when leaving the room. The white team member would then do one of three things: make no comment, make a moderately racist comment, or make a blatant and vulgar racist comment. In many cases, the experiencer added an insulting comment of his or her own. However, in all three scenarios, the experiencers reported very little distress over what they had witnessed.

The forecasters, on the other hand, were merely asked to predict their response to each of the three scenarios described above. In both the moderate and extreme scenarios, the forecasters reported they would feel a great deal of distress—much more distress than the experiencers reported actually feeling. The results of this study surprised the researchers. Psychology professor Kerry Kawakami, the lead researcher, explained, "Some people might think that they're very egalitarian and they don't have to deal with their prejudices, and that it's not related to them at all, when in actual fact they may hold these hidden biases." He added, "This study … suggests that there are still really a lot of negative associations with blacks. People are willing to tolerate racism and not stand up against it."[13]

Part of the reason racism is tolerated may be that white people often find it difficult to recognize that they have privilege. There are thousands of ways white people benefit from the color of their skin, ranging from minor—for example, seeing more white people than people of color in movies—to major—for instance, not having to worry that any encounter with the police may turn violent. White people tend to get defensive when asked to think about the ways their privilege benefits them; many believe people of color are too sensitive to racial slights and that when people tell them they have privilege, they are implying that white people do not ever have to work hard. This is untrue; many white people work hard to achieve success. However, people of color often have to work harder than white people to achieve the same successes, and it is important for white people

People of color often have to apply for more jobs than white people do before they get a response.

to remember this when they think of criticizing someone who must struggle against racism every day.

As writer Molefi Kete Asante explained, racial discrimination persists in society in both overt and subtle ways:

> *We [black people] walk into an automobile showroom and we are quoted higher prices than whites; we work as cooks in restaurants where whites with less skill and less time in the job are paid more; we step into employment agencies and they direct us away from jobs, high school counselors direct us away from African American Studies courses where we can learn about our history and culture. We are told that there are no apartments available, but when our white friends call the same agency they are told there are several apartments available.*[14]

White people sometimes become upset when groups are created specifically for people of color. They claim that these groups do more to promote racism than erase it because people of color are setting themselves apart and pointing out their own race, rather than trying to combine with white culture so that race is no longer an issue. However, these arguments suggest that white people would rather make race disappear than talk about it. They may speak of not wanting to have it "shoved in their faces," forgetting that for people of color, white culture is all around them all the time. Additionally, they do not take into account the fact that people of color often need these groups to connect with people who have shared values and experiences in a place where they feel safe.

In 2015, a group called POC Yoga offered yoga classes for people of color of all ages, genders, sexual orientations, and athletic abilities. The group respectfully asked white people not to attend. After POC Yoga was criticized and called racist by a talk show host for excluding white people, one of the founders, Teresa Wang, received hundreds of angry e-mails, phone calls, and death threats from white people. According to Joe R. Feagin, professor of sociology at Texas A&M University,

> *Those death threats alone illustrate exactly why people of color need safe spaces … Racism is still extraordinarily widespread in this country and does great harm to people of color … therefore it is not only*

logical but necessary that people of color create safe spaces away from whites in which to deal with the stresses of racism and build up strategies to resist.[15]

It may never be possible to completely eliminate racism from society, but to at least reduce it, it is necessary for white people to listen to the voices of people of color and try to understand their point of view.

The Importance of Intersectionality

Because issues such as race, gender, and class are so complex, people tend to discuss one at a time. However, in real life, all of these issues influence each other. This influence is known as intersectionality, and it means that because people of color, women, members of the LGBTQIA community, and people who live in poverty all experience disadvantage, a poor Latina woman will experience more disadvantage than a wealthy Latina woman, a poor white woman, or a poor Latino man.

It is sometimes difficult for people to remember intersectionality, so exclusion sometimes happens even within social justice movements. For instance, the Women's March on Washington in January 2017 was originally organized completely by white women. After receiving criticism for this, they made an effort to include women of color. According to Ruth Enid Zambrana, director of the Consortium on Race, Gender and Ethnicity at the University of Maryland, "White women need to recognize that gender isn't a single category. There is a need to acknowledge underrepresented women and domestic groups that have different histories and are at a tremendous disadvantage."[1]

1. Quoted in Alia E. Dastagir, "What Is Intersectional Feminism? A Look at the Term You May Be Hearing a Lot," *USA Today*, January 19, 2017. www.usatoday.com/story/news/2017/01/19/feminism-intersectionality-racism-sexism-class/96633750/.

CHAPTER 2

Factors of Racism

The causes of racism are wide-ranging and complex. Some people, called white supremacists, have a strong belief that whites are better than other races. Others have learned negative stereotypes about certain races that they have never bothered to correct by doing research or getting to know someone of that race. Many racist beliefs are born out of fear and ignorance, and facing those beliefs is often an uncomfortable experience. Even people who support racial justice and equality often have prejudices they do not know about until they suddenly encounter a situation they have never faced before. Racism is perpetuated, or continued, by people who are not willing to deal with the discomfort of facing their prejudices.

Fear and Ignorance

Racism begins with the idea that humans can be separated into different groups based on perceived physical differences, such as skin color, facial features, and hair texture. These differences are the basis for what is commonly thought of as "race." Long ago, it was believed that people with different features were genetically different from one another. Today, however, with advances in human genetics, scientists now know that people of different races are not biologically separate. In fact, human beings, no matter where they are from or what their perceived race is, are essentially the same in their genetic makeup. Race is merely a social concept.

However, people continue to separate others into distinct "races" and form ideas and opinions about what each race is like. This is due in part to the human tendency to form stereotypes—oversimplified ways of categorizing other people. The need for a way to put various people into general groups most likely arose in the earliest days of human existence, when knowing which group, family, or tribe one belonged to was necessary for survival. Stereotypes may provide people with a shorthand way to categorize others, but they can be harmful. They can lead to the belief that because certain people are classified as a group, then they must all be alike. This is especially harmful when a stereotype involves negative traits being associated with the group. For example, various groups of people throughout history have been viewed as dishonest, lazy, stupid, violent, and a host of other negative attributes. The belief that whole groups of people hold undesirable traits can lead to racial prejudice—an unfavorable judgment about other people based on the color of their skin.

There is no specific gene for race. Skin color, eye shape, and other physical features are determined by many different genes.

WHITE IS THE DEFAULT

"In this country American means white. Everybody else has to hyphenate."–Toni Morrison, author

Quoted in Maria Chavez, Jessica L. Lavariega Monforti, and Melissa R. Michelson, *Living the Dream: New Immigration Policies and the Lives of Undocumented Latino Youth*. New York, NY: Taylor & Francis, 2015, p. 16.

Stereotypes and racial prejudice can lead to a mistrust of people from another racial group. Psychologist Beverly Daniel Tatum explained that racism can begin in childhood and stem from a lack of experience with anyone who is different from oneself. In her book, "*Why Are All the Black Kids Sitting Together in the Cafeteria?*": *And Other Conversations About Race*, Tatum wrote,

> *The impact of racism begins early. Even in our preschool years, we are exposed to misinformation about people different from ourselves. Many of us grew up in neighborhoods where we had limited opportunities to interact with people different from our own families. When I ask my college students, "How many of you grew up in neighborhoods where most of the people were from the same racial group as your own?" almost every hand goes up. There is still a great deal of social segregation in our communities. Consequently, most of the early information we receive about "others"—people racially, religiously, or socioeconomically different from ourselves—does not come as the result of firsthand experience. The secondhand information we do receive has often been distorted, shaped by cultural stereotypes, and left incomplete.*[16]

The American Psychological Association (APA) has said that it is human nature for people to avoid things that make them feel anxious or uncomfortable. This avoidance contributes to many people's lack of experience with people of another race. The APA explained,

> *Our stereotypes of other groups … often lead to feelings of anxiety when we encounter the members of [that] group. One of the oldest insights of psychology is that a main way we deal with anxiety is through avoidance: We simply avoid contact with individuals by crossing the*

> *street, turning our heads, talking to someone else, hiring someone else for a job, striking up friendships with someone else we feel more comfortable with, sitting down at the lunch table with those who seem to be more like us.*[17]

Such misinformation and lack of contact can reinforce negative stereotypes and lead to inaccurate assumptions about anyone who is a different race. These assumptions may then lead to fear that a person's life will be negatively impacted by a racial group. This fear and mistrust of others goes hand in hand with prejudice and can lead to a person developing negative and hostile attitudes toward others based solely on their race. Such attitudes can also lead to a belief that one race is inherently, or naturally, "better" than another.

A Belief in Superiority

Racial prejudice often develops from one race's sense of superiority over another. When the first European settlers came to what is now the United States, they believed the land they encountered belonged to them simply because they had landed there. They viewed the Native Americans who were living there as savages because they lived in different types of shelters, had different customs, and wore different clothing than the Europeans. In the early United States, the belief that black people were an inferior race was the cornerstone of slavery. Even after slavery ended, generations of prejudice encouraged white people to view themselves as better than black people.

Many white people also have a bias against people from other countries. It is a common belief that immigrants, especially those who come to the United States illegally, keep white Americans unemployed by taking jobs that would otherwise have gone to them. However, many of the jobs undocumented workers do are jobs that most American citizens do not want and do not apply for, such as picking fruit and cleaning houses.

People who do not speak English well or speak it with an accent are also looked down on by fluent English speakers because they automatically assume someone who does not speak their language is not as intelligent as they are. The TV show

Race versus Religion

Sometimes people confuse race and religion because so many people of a particular race also follow a particular religion. The two religions this occurs with most commonly are Judaism and Islam. Anti-Semitism is the term for prejudice against Jews, while Islamophobia is the comparable term for prejudice against Muslims. Judaism and Islam are religions that anyone of any race can convert to, but they are most often practiced by people who share a common heritage. People who do not belong to either of these religions but appear to have the same features as someone who does may also be discriminated against. Sociologist Stuart Hall called this cultural racism, which "happens when certain people perceive their beliefs and customs as being culturally superior to the beliefs and customs of other groups of people."[1] Since race is a concept that was made up by society, it is possible for the definition of race to shift over time. However, as of 2017, race is still used mainly to separate people based on skin color and other physical features.

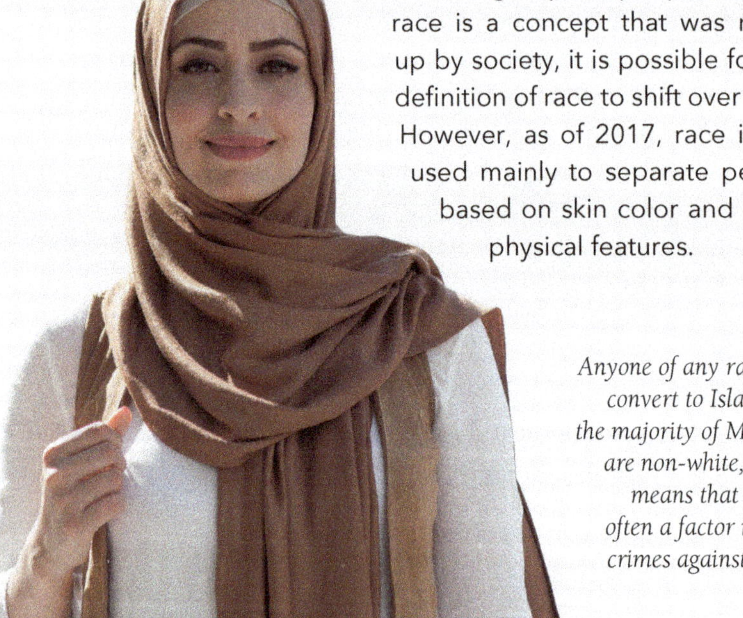

Anyone of any race can convert to Islam, but the majority of Muslims are non-white, which means that race is often a factor in hate crimes against them.

1. Craig Considine, "Muslims Aren't a Race, So I Can't Be Racist, Right? Wrong," *Huffington Post*, November 19, 2015. www.huffingtonpost.com/craig-considine/muslims-are-not-a-race_b_8591660.html.

Modern Family pointed out this bias in a scene where the character Gloria, who is a native Spanish-speaker from Colombia, was having an argument with her husband. She said, "Do you know how frustrating it is to have to translate everything in my head before I say it? To have people laugh in my face because I'm struggling to find the words? You should try talking in my shoes for one mile." When her husband said, "I think you meant …" Gloria responded, "I know what I meant to mean. Do you know how smart I am in Spanish? Of course you don't."[18]

Gloria on Modern Family *is played by actress Sofia Vergara, who, like her character, is from Colombia.*

People of color have historically had little political or cultural power in the United States. They were typically relegated to second-class status and had no access to the education available to most whites. Although U.S. laws state that race is not a barrier to running for political office, people of color are less likely to be elected because of the attitude of white superiority that still exists in the country at both a conscious and unconscious level.

Part of the reason this attitude of white superiority continues to exist is that it allows white people to feel good about their own identity and that of their group. Being part of the dominant group in a society—or the "in" group—can lead some people to believe that they actually are superior in some way to members of the "out" group. In addition, members of the "in" group enjoy certain benefits and advantages. The APA explained why prejudices and stereotypes that give privilege to one group over another often remain unexamined:

> *Because stereotypes may help us feel better about ourselves, we avoid challenging these stereotypes. In other words, we become defensive and protective of our worldviews and only reluctantly question our deepest assumptions. And these worldviews help protect not only our self-esteem, but also real-world privileges and benefits that accrue to us as members of an in group. For example, racist discrimination by banks that hurts African American communities by limiting mortgages to these areas also benefits White neighborhoods by making more money available to them … So, maintaining our prejudiced views of others allows us to feel better about our own group and to avoid challenging unfair social practices that benefit us.*[19]

When these negative racist ideas and prejudicial attitudes remain intact, it enables white people to maintain the power and advantages they hold in society. This is known as "white privilege." Some people—for example, members of white supremacy groups—are aware of their desire to keep white privilege intact. Others may never have stopped to think about the fact that they enjoy certain advantages because they are white. Whether people acknowledge it or not, white superiority remains a factor in interactions between people of color and white people today.

RACISM IS TAUGHT

"Racism is learned behavior. The way in which a white child behaves toward an ethnic group is a direct reflection of their parents' attitude about race. If a child hears his or her parents vocalizing racial stereotypes, the child learns to identify everyone in that group by those labels."–S. Maxx Mahaffey, author

S. Maxx Mahaffey, "Is Racism Taught or Learned?," Helium. www.helium.com/items/882142-is-racism-taught-or-learned.

Encounters with Police

Racial profiling is a method of using racial or ethnic characteristics to determine whether a person is likely to commit a crime. Law enforcement agencies around the world have relied on racial profiling for years to predict who will or will not commit a crime. For example, since the terrorist attacks on the United States on September 11, 2001, fears of more attacks have led to greater security screening of Arab and Middle Eastern people, as well as those with a similar skin tone, such as Indian and other Southeast Asian people. These people are stopped, searched, and sometimes barred from boarding airplanes. Millions of people of color experience racial profiling on a daily basis. Security officials argue that these tactics are necessary to protect people, but critics say it is unfair and leads to further racial prejudice: Racial profiling reinforces the negative stereotype of people of color as untrustworthy, which contributes to such attitudes continuing in society.

Many times, racial profiling is unjustified. In 2017, after President Trump ordered a temporary immigration ban on people traveling from seven Muslim-majority countries, a brown-skinned woman named Aravinda Pillalamarri, who is a U.S. citizen and lives in Bel Air, Maryland, was stopped by police while she was out for a walk. The police said someone who lived in the neighborhood had reported her as a suspicious person. "I had just come out for a walk, so I didn't have my ID. And he said, 'Why don't you have ID? Are you here illegally?'"

she told reporters. The Bel Air police denied that it was a case of racial profiling, saying, "They were trying to figure out why there was some hesitation to provide identification ... That's why he asked if she was illegal."[20]

The racial profiling of black drivers has become so common in the United States that a phrase and an acronym has been invented

Black drivers are more likely to get pulled over than white ones. Sometimes these traffic stops escalate to violence.

to describe it. "Driving While Black," or DWB, may be a symptom of racial prejudice. The fact that it happens so often may also contribute to negative societal perceptions of black people. In other words, people assume that black people must be criminals because of how often they get pulled over, even though many times they have not done anything to deserve getting pulled over.

Sometimes a police encounter that would be routine for a white person turns dangerous or deadly for a person of color. In Minnesota in 2016, a 32-year-old black man named Philando Castile was shot by police after they stopped him because his taillight was broken. The officer asked Castile to show his identification, and when Castile reached for his wallet, the officer shot him, assuming that he was reaching for a gun. Mark Dayton, the governor of Minnesota "said he found both the shooting and the aftermath 'absolutely appalling at all levels,' noting in particular that no first aid was provided to Castile, while other police officers did attend to the officer who fired the shots."[21] This is one of numerous incidents of police brutality that have been in the news for the past several years.

Black Lives Matter

In 2012, a black teen named Trayvon Martin was shot and killed by George Zimmerman, a Hispanic neighborhood watch captain in Sanford, Florida, where Martin's father lived. Zimmerman called the police to report Martin as a suspicious person, then disregarded the police's instructions not to get out of his car or engage with Martin. Zimmerman shot Martin, claiming self-defense. However, due to evidence that suggested Zimmerman had provoked Martin into fighting him, Zimmerman was arrested and tried for murder. Although he was eventually found not guilty, many people were outraged over the shooting, which was widely regarded to be motivated by Martin's race.

The killing of Trayvon Martin was widely considered to be racially motivated.

In response to the shooting, many people began using the hashtag #BlackLivesMatter on social media. The movement grew as more instances of police brutality against black people were reported in the news. An organization was founded and now has chapters in 31 cities across the United States. Rallies and protests have been organized to bring attention to the fact that black people still face racism in the United States and to bring about changes to policies that negatively affect black people.

Some people have criticized BLM, saying that its focus on race divides the country rather than bringing it together. Counter-protest hashtags such as #AllLivesMatter have been used on social media to argue against what some people see as black people claiming that their lives are the only ones that matter. However, BLM supporters point out that while it is true that all lives matter, their campaign is highlighting the fact that their lives are often treated as less important than the lives of white people. American civil rights activist DeRay Mckesson explained this by saying, "I would never go to a breast cancer rally and yell out, 'Colon cancer matters!'"[22]

Unconscious Bias

People often respond to one another based on attitudes they hold about each other's race—attitudes they may hold at an unconscious level. In fact, one of the main motivations for racial prejudice may actually be deeply ingrained racist attitudes that people are unaware they hold. Few people would admit to holding a racial bias; fewer still would describe themselves as racists. However, leading universities have created a series of online tests that measure people's tendency toward bias or prejudice, with surprising results.

The Implicit Association Test (IAT) is designed to measure the speed with which people categorize images they are shown. There are several types of IATs that measure bias in various areas, such as gender, age, and race. The racial IAT asks test takers to quickly categorize faces, black and white, that appear on the computer screen using certain words, such as "evil," "glorious," or "wonderful." Because those taking the test are encouraged to work fast, they give little conscious thought to their answers.

Controversy over the Confederate Flag

When the South tried to secede from the North during the American Civil War and form the Confederate States of America, it created a battle flag for the new country. Even after the South lost the war, this flag remained a symbol of pride for some Southerners, and some people defend it by saying that it symbolizes their cultural heritage. However, because one reason for the South's secession was the desire for slavery to remain legal, the flag also symbolizes a belief in white superiority. This is especially true when it is seen in northern states, where people have no cultural connection to the flag.

In 2015, a white man named Dylann Roof killed nine black people in a church in Charleston, South Carolina. In response, people began calling for the Confederate flag to be removed from the South Carolina State House. Additionally, people tried to get stores such as Wal-Mart and Amazon to stop selling products that have the flag on them. The flag no longer flies at the State House, but products can still be found in some stores and online.

Many places have banned this flag as a symbol of hatred against black people.

What IAT analysts have discovered is that the majority of those who take the test show a bias toward white faces. Even some black respondents showed a preference for white faces.

Malcolm Gladwell, the son of a white father and a black mother, wrote extensively about IATs in his book, *Blink*. After taking the test himself, he felt slightly embarrassed by his own results. Even though he is well educated and multiracial, he discovered he had prejudices he was not even aware of. After taking the test four times, Gladwell was rated as having a "moderate automatic preference for whites."[23] This shows that attitudes on race are based on both the biases people are aware of and those that are unconscious, or hidden, even from themselves.

A HISTORY OF SLAVERY

"Never forget that we were enslaved in this country longer than we have been free. Never forget that for 250 years black people were born into chains—whole generations followed by more generations who knew nothing but chains."
—Ta-Nehisi Coates, author

Ta-Nehisi Coates, *Between the World and Me*. New York, NY: Spiegel & Grau, 2015, p. 70.

Race and Poverty

Because racism makes it harder for people of color to get certain jobs, many are stuck in a cycle of poverty. Being poor makes it difficult to save money because there are many things people must pay for on a regular basis to survive, including food, gas or bus fare to get to work, clothing, shoes, rent, and utilities (heating, water, and electricity bills). Any large, unexpected expenses, such as medical bills, can drive already impoverished people into deep debt. Many people unfairly look down on others who have less-prestigious jobs, earn less money, drive less-expensive cars, or live in smaller homes than they do. This can be a powerful factor for racism when so many people of color live in poverty. According to the University of Michigan's National Poverty

Center (NPC), "Poverty rates for blacks and Hispanics greatly exceed the national average. In 2014, 26.2 percent of blacks and 23.6 percent of Hispanics were poor, compared to 10.1 percent of non-Hispanic whites and 12 percent of Asians."[24]

People of color who come to the United States from other countries often have less money and have less choice in jobs than American citizens. According to the NPC, "In 2014, 18.5 percent of foreign-born residents lived in poverty, compared to 14.2 percent of residents born in the United States. Foreign-born, noncitizens had an even higher incidence of poverty, at a rate of 24.2 percent."[25] Living in poverty is a vicious cycle, so it is often hard for people of color to save money.

Native Americans are also more likely to live in poverty, mainly as a result of government policies that have been directed

Racism often makes it hard for people of color to get high-paying jobs, but low-paying jobs keep them stuck in a cycle of poverty.

against them since the first white colonists arrived in what is now the United States. Their land is owned and managed by the federal government, which means they are not able to make their own economic decisions. The process for approval of projects to improve the economy is often slow; according to *Forbes*, "On Indian lands, companies must go through at least four federal agencies and 49 steps to acquire a permit for energy development. Off reservation, it takes only four steps. This bureaucracy prevents tribes from capitalizing on their resources."[26] The government also controls payments that are made to reservations and sometimes does not pay them everything they are owed. This means Native Americans have less money to use for their schools and other public institutions. According to the Pew Research Center, "Native Americans have a higher poverty and unemployment rate when compared with the national average, but the rates are comparable to those of blacks and Hispanics."[27]

In addition, people of color are sometimes blamed for their own predicament. This is known as blaming the victim, and it comes about because humans like to believe the world is fair and bad things only happen to those who deserve it. Therefore, if the world is fair, then those who are in a bad situation must have done something to deserve their misfortune. Similar to blaming victims for their own problems is the idea that if people just tried hard enough, they could make their situation better. These ideas play a part in racist attitudes about people of color being poor because they are lazy or do not care enough about their situation to do something about it. In reality, the vast majority of people who live in poverty work extremely hard, often holding two or more jobs just to make ends meet. Victim blaming is something that is deeply ingrained in society, and many people may not realize they hold such an attitude.

Knowing that many people of color live in poverty can lead people to assume that all people of color live in poverty. Sometimes this leads to discrimination such as refusing to serve a person of color in a store based on the assumption that the person does not have money to pay for what they are looking at. Other times, it leads people to say or do offensive things that they believe are nice or helpful, such as telling a person of color where the nearest soup kitchen is or offering to buy them a meal. This is offensive because it assumes that any person of color must be homeless or poor, when in reality, many people of color overcome the odds that are stacked against them to achieve high status and wealth.

For Asians, unlike many other people of color, the stereotypes are generally positive. In the past, they were discriminated against with policies such as the Chinese Exclusion Act, which banned Chinese immigrants from 1882 to 1943, as well as the forced internment, or imprisonment, of Japanese-American citizens after the Japanese attack on Pearl Harbor in 1941. Over time, perceptions changed, and today, Asians are seen as hardworking, intelligent, and successful. However, this does not mean they do not suffer from racism. According to Josh Ishimatsu, deputy director of the National Coalition for Asian Pacific American Community Development, "There's a presumption that all [Asian-Americans and Pacific Islanders] are rich and educated ... The people who

are not don't have much in the way of services available—they're just not known or seen."[28]

Being seen as high-achieving can make it difficult for Asians—including East Asians from China, Japan, and Korea, as well as Southeast Asians from places such as India, Cambodia, Pakistan, and the Philippines—to get access to the services they need when they live in poverty or to be taken seriously when they speak about the problems they face. White people also may not see stereotypes of Asians as racist because the associations are generally positive, which makes it difficult to make people see that they need to change their perceptions.

The reasons for racism are varied and complex. Some are centuries old, while others have come about more recently. Many stem from unconscious attitudes that people hold and never think about. However, racism is embedded in society, even at the unconscious level.

Thousands of Japanese-American citizens lost their homes and possessions during World War II when the government forced them to relocate to internment camps.

CHAPTER 3

Racism in Society

Despite laws that have been created with the aim of fighting racism, society still suffers from racist practices. In many cases, it is difficult to prove that any sort of discrimination is taking place; for instance, an employer who hires a white person over a person of color may say that the white person was more qualified. This may or may not be true, but since job candidates do not see each other's résumés, there is no way for a candidate to be sure. Sometimes laws actively work against the interests of people of color, especially in the case of Native Americans.

Some practices are not illegal but are still racist and can have a damaging effect on people of color. Since white people are the majority in Western society, beauty products, dolls, actors, models, and many other aspects of Western culture are aimed at them. This often sends a message to people of color that they are not as important as white people. Many white people, even those with good intentions, are so used to seeing these things that they have stopped noticing how common they are until the imbalance is pointed out to them.

Cultural Appropriation

Many white people do not view the practice of cultural appropriation as racist. Cultural appropriation "involves members of a dominant group exploiting the culture of less privileged groups—often with little understanding of the latter's history, experience and traditions."[29] This may include hairstyles, clothing, musical styles, or other aspects of a particular culture. As the world becomes increasingly more connected through fast travel and the Internet, some exchange of cultural ideas is going to take place. However, it can become a problem when white people profit from the cultures of people of color or use their culture in ways that are offensive.

One example of cultural appropriation that has sparked much controversy is when white people wear Native American headdresses and war paint, which is especially common at music festivals. Many people wear them because they like the way they look, but Native Americans have made it clear that this practice is offensive for a number of reasons. According to the website Native Appropriations, one reason is that people who are not Native American are pretending to be, which is similar to blackface—the racist practice of putting on black makeup to pretend to be a black person. Another is that warbonnets and feathers have a strong spiritual meaning to Native American cultures, so when people who have no ties to the culture wear them, it shows a lack of respect for Native Americans and their practices. A third reason is that the image of a Native American wearing those items

> *is one that has been created and perpetuated by Hollywood and only bears minimal resemblance to traditional regalia of Plains tribes. It furthers the stereotype that Native peoples are one monolithic culture, when in fact there are 500+ distinct tribes with their own cultures. It also places Native people in the historic past, as something that cannot exist in modern society. We don't walk around in ceremonial attire [every day], but we still exist and are Native.*[30]

Many Native Americans find it offensive when white people wear Native American headdresses.

Some people feel that cultural appropriation is not a problem because there is now so much overlap among different cultures; for instance, many non-Japanese people eat sushi. However, cultural appropriation is a problem "when the new adoption is void of the significance that it was supposed to have—it strips the religious, historical and cultural context of something and makes it mass-marketable."[31] Any time an object that holds significance for one culture is treated as a decoration by another culture, it is offensive.

The Problem of Whitewashing

Whitewashing is a term that can refer to several things. One is when a photo of a person of color is edited to look like he or she has lighter skin than in reality. Another is when a white person is cast as a person of color in a movie or TV show. One example of whitewashing happens frequently in beauty magazines. Dark-skinned women who pose for photo shoots are often seen on the covers of magazines such as *Vanity Fair*, *Vogue*, and *Elle* with noticeably lighter skin. The magazines often claim that it is the lighting at the photo shoot that gives this effect, but people who work in the photo industry have countered that claim by saying that photographers have special equipment that prevents this from happening. In reality, it is most likely true that these photographs have been digitally edited to make the actresses appear lighter. This is damaging because it contributes to a perception of beauty that is Eurocentric—focusing on the way white European women look. A Eurocentric standard of beauty may cause dark-skinned women to feel that they are less beautiful than women with white or light skin.

This attempt to minimize or erase people of color can also be seen on book covers. Sometimes a book that has a main character of color will have a cover that features a white person, someone who could be seen as white, or someone whose face is hidden. In some cases, publishers have changed their covers in response to outrage from authors and readers. For instance, the book *Liar* by Justine Larbalestier describes the main character, Micah, as a black girl who wears her hair naturally. When the book was first released, however, the cover featured a black-and-white photo of a girl who was clearly white with straight hair. In response to backlash by the public, the publishing company changed the cover to show a black girl with curly hair.

Another example of whitewashing is the 2016 film *Gods of Egypt*. As the title makes clear, the movie was set in Egypt, but the cast was almost entirely white, so it received much criticism. The director and the film company apologized to the public for the choice of casting, but it was too late to change anything. Another is *Ghost in the Shell*, a 2017 movie starring Scarlett Johansson. Rupert Sanders, the movie's director, stated that he cast Johansson because she was the best actress for the part, but many people were upset that a white actress was cast as a Japanese character. Some people feel that it does not matter who is cast in a movie as long as the acting is good, but whitewashing makes it harder for people of color to get acting roles and contributes to the lack of diversity in popular culture.

Ghost in the Shell *was criticized for casting Scarlett Johansson as the main character because many people viewed it as an example of whitewashing.*

A Lack of Diversity at Award Shows

Whitewashing makes it difficult for actors of color to get roles, but even when they do break into the industry, they often have trouble getting recognized for their work. In 2016, the hashtag #OscarsSoWhite began trending on social media, highlighting the fact that for two years in a row, not one single person of color had been nominated for an Oscar as a lead or supporting actor. Even though some movies featuring actors of color had been highly praised by critics, the Academy of Motion Picture Arts and Sciences—the organization that nominates actors for Oscars, often referred to simply as the Academy—had overlooked all of them. In some cases, even when a movie featured people of color, the nomination went to a white person who had worked on the film. For instance, the movie *Straight Outta Compton* starred mainly black people, but its Oscar nomination went to its white screenwriters.

Because of this lack of diversity, many actors and filmmakers, such as Spike Lee, Will Smith, Jada Pinkett Smith, and Michael Moore chose to boycott the 2016 Oscars. Some people in the industry did not boycott but did speak out for more diversity in Hollywood. Others dismissed the issue, claiming that the best people were nominated for the awards regardless of race. However, in response to the outrage, the governing board of the Academy, which is currently made up primarily of white men, pledged to double the amount of people of color and women on the board by 2020. In 2017, the movie

AGE DOES NOT MATTER

"Age tells us far less about an individual's likelihood of expressing racist sentiments than factors like education, geography and race."
–Sean McElwee, research associate

Sean McElwee, "The Hidden Racism of Young White Americans," PBS *NewsHour*, March 24, 2015. www.pbs.org/newshour/updates/americas-racism-problem-far-complicated-think/.

Moonlight became the first movie directed by a black person to win the Oscar for Best Picture. This was not a direct response to the #OscarsSoWhite controversy, but people were happy to see that a movie with black actors and directors was given the credit most felt it deserved.

Creating Equal Opportunity

The Academy's promise could be considered one example of affirmative action—a policy of giving special preference to people because of their race, ethnicity, or gender. The goal of affirmative action is to provide equal opportunity and to encourage—even demand—diversity in the workplace, in schools, in government, and in other arenas. Affirmative action can also be implemented to make amends for past wrongs, such as slavery or other racial injustices.

Affirmative action is controversial in the United States. The 14th Amendment to the Constitution, which was ratified in 1868, protects all American citizens, regardless of race, gender, or religion, from discrimination. People of color, however, continued to be legally discriminated against for another hundred years. In the mid-20th century, white Americans still received preferential treatment in virtually all areas of life, including hiring practices, job promotions, wages, housing, and university admissions. The lack of access to a quality education made it even harder for people of color to compete against white people in the workplace. The unemployment rate for black people in the early 1960s was twice that of white people, and black men earned barely more than half of what white men earned. As a consequence, 55 percent of black people were living in poverty in 1960.

President Lyndon B. Johnson was an outspoken champion of civil rights for black people in particular. In a speech he delivered in 1965 at Howard University, a predominantly black school in Washington, D.C., Johnson explained why he believed that protective measures such as affirmative action were necessary to increase equality:

Hamilton: An American Musical

Hamilton: An American Musical was created by Lin-Manuel Miranda, an American playwright and actor of Puerto Rican descent. It premiered off-Broadway in February 2015, but was so popular that it quickly moved to Broadway. Tickets were difficult to get, and available seats cost up to $900.

One thing that sets *Hamilton* apart from other shows is its diverse cast. The only major part played by a white actor in the original Broadway production was King George III. Some claim this is discrimination against white actors, but most note that this is simply how casting works–the director is allowed to choose the people he or she thinks best represent the story being told. The casting call originally asked nonwhite actors to audition; however, Actors' Equity, the theater actors' union, said that although the show can specify the race, gender, and age of each character, the auditions must be open to anyone of any race. In response to this criticism, the language of the casting call was changed to reflect the fact that white actors were welcome to try out.

One of Miranda's goals was to give black, Asian, and Latinx actors a chance to take roles that are traditionally denied to them because of the color of their skin, and in this, he succeeded. According to the *Huffington Post*, the show "is a musical that lives and breathes hip-hop. Its music and diverse cast, juxtaposed with the story of a country just beginning to find its voice, perfectly reflect the complex racial history and identity of America."[1]

1. Zeba Blay, "No, the 'Hamilton' Casting Call for 'Non-White' Actors Is Not Reverse Racism," *Huffington Post*, last updated November 22, 2016. www.huffingtonpost.com/entry/no-the-hamilton-casting-call-for-non-white-actors-is-not-reverse-racism_us_56fd2c83e4b0daf53aeed9b9.

Hamilton: An American Musical, created by Lin-Manuel Miranda (third from left), was an immediate success.

> *You do not take a person who, for years, has been hobbled by chains and liberate him, bring him up to the starting line of a race and then say, "you are free to compete with all the others," and still justly believe that you have been completely fair. Thus it is not enough just to open the gates of opportunity. All our citizens must have the ability to walk through those gates.*[32]

In an effort to combat the racial inequality that existed in the United States, Johnson signed the Civil Rights Act of 1964. This act prohibits discrimination on the basis of race or sex in the workplace, public facilities, union membership, and

Affirmative action requires some companies to hire a certain number of women and people of color.

federally funded programs. The act also established the EEOC, which led the way to the use of affirmative action. With affirmative action, people of color were to be given preferential treatment in hiring practices and university admissions. Employers were ordered not only to cease discriminating against people of color, but to actively hire them.

After Johnson left office, following presidents amended affirmative action, and dozens of court cases have either challenged or upheld the government policy. Writing in support of affirmative action in 1978, Harry Blackmun, associate justice of the U.S. Supreme Court from 1970 to 1994, said, "In order to get beyond racism, we must first take account of race. There is no other way. And in order to treat some persons equally, we must treat them differently."[33]

Controversy Surrounding Affirmative Action

Thanks to affirmative action programs, people of color found themselves being hired for jobs that formerly were closed to them and admitted to universities that formerly barred them. Any organization that accepts funding from the government is legally required to hire or admit a certain percentage of women and people of color. This requirement, known as the quota system, remains one of the most controversial aspects of affirmative action, and mandated affirmative action based on race has come under heavy criticism in recent years. These critics call affirmative action "reverse discrimination" that unfairly affects white Americans who, despite better qualifications, may not be selected because they are not a person of color. However, these accusations do not take into account the fact that white people are often given more opportunities throughout their lives to attain those qualifications.

For Asians, affirmative action policies can sometimes be harmful. Because of the belief that they are the "model minority," they are excluded from affirmative action programs but are still often passed over in favor of white candidates—often ones with lower test scores or fewer qualifications. When Asians complain about this unfair treatment, people often blame affirmative action, saying that if black and Latinx people were not given preferential treatment, Asians would have a better chance. However, this argument overlooks the fact that white people still have the best chance of any race of getting the positions they are seeking.

Some argue that the United States has changed dramatically since affirmative action was first enacted, and therefore, the race-based policy is no longer necessary. Instead, they believe affirmative action would serve a better purpose if used to help the economically needy, regardless of race. "As this generation rises, race-based discrimination needs to go," *New York Times* columnist Ross Douthat wrote in 2009. "The explicit scale-tipping in college admissions should give way to class-based affirmative action; the de facto racial preferences required of employers by anti-discrimination law should disappear."[34]

Another vocal opponent of affirmative action is Ward Connerly, an African American political activist. To Connerly, the best evidence that affirmative action is outdated was the election of President Barack Obama. "The whole argument in favor of race preferences is that there is 'institutional racism'… in American life, and you need affirmative action to level the playing field," Connerly said. "How can you say there is institutional racism when people in Nebraska vote for a guy who is a self-identified black man?"[35]

Many people agreed with Connerly that Obama's election proved racism was no longer an issue. However, many other people did not approve of Obama's presidency—some legitimately disagreed with his policies, while others simply disliked him because of the color of his skin. Some consider Trump's election to be retaliation by whites against blacks. According to CNN, "Dramatic racial progress in America is inevitably followed by a white backlash, or 'whitelash.' Reconstruction in the 19th century was followed by a century of Jim Crow. The Civil Rights Movement of the 1950s and '60s was followed by President Ronald Reagan and the rise of the religious right."[36] CNN commentator Van Jones, who used the word "whitelash" on television after the election, later clarified that he was speaking specifically about alt-right and neo-Nazi Trump voters.

Sports Teams and Racist Names

The Washington Redskins are a professional football team with a controversial name and symbol, which is the face of a Native American man. Some people defend the name and logo, saying they are intended to honor Native Americans. They also say it is a beloved tradition and that fans would be upset if the name changed. However, critics, including many Native Americans, say the term "redskin" is offensive and often used as a slur. They state that using a person as a sports mascot is offensive as well, since mascots are traditionally objects, animals, or mythological creatures. It is clear that many Native Americans do not view the name and logo as an honor, regardless of how it may have been intended.

Other sports teams that have also received criticism are the Cleveland Indians, the Kansas City Chiefs, the Chicago Blackhawks, and the Atlanta Braves. In 2005, the APA urged all sports teams with Native American names or logos to change them, based on "a growing body of social science literature that shows the harmful effects of racial stereotyping and inaccurate racial portrayals, including the particularly harmful effects of American Indian sports mascots on the social identity development and self-esteem of American Indian young people."[1]

1. "Summary of the APA Resolution Recommending Retirement of American Indian Mascots," American Psychological Association. www.apa.org/pi/oema/resources/indian-mascots.aspx.

The Rise of the Alt-Right

After the civil rights movement, the United States slowly moved toward a culture that discouraged obvious racism. It was frowned upon for people to use racial slurs or make comments that implied people of color were inferior to whites. However, in private and sometimes in public, many people—most of whom were white—still said these things to others who agreed with their views and complained about what they called

PC (politically correct) culture. They wanted to speak freely without being told they were being offensive.

During Trump's campaign, when he also complained about PC culture and said things that many people regarded as offensive, a group of his supporters calling themselves the alternative right, or alt-right, became even more vocal. The members of the alt-right moevement say many things, especially online, that are racist, sexist, and anti-Semitic. When people challenge them, they accuse their critics of being brainwashed by the liberal media and proclaim that they have the right to free speech in America. The alt-right has been compared to the Nazi Party in pre-World War II Germany because of its views.

EQUALITY REQUIRES ACTION

"So we must recognise that we will not succeed in tackling racism without tackling all forms of discrimination, prejudice and inequality. We have to redouble our efforts to promote greater equality for all, and combine that with action to target the specific problems faced by particular groups."
–John Denham, former member of British Parliament

"John Denham: Tackling Racism Means Tackling All Forms of Discrimination," *Independent*, January 14, 2010. www.independent.co.uk/opinion/commentators/ john-denham-tackling-racism-means-tackling-all-forms-of-discrimination-1868357.html.

Trump's popularity with the alt-right arose mainly due to his campaign promises to prevent suspected Muslim extremists and undocumented immigrants from entering the country. Members of the alt-right see these and similar policies as a way of preventing white people from being discriminated against; they see equality with people of color and women as a threat because it would mean losing their privilege. Although equality means that everyone has the same opportunities, the alt-right sees it as a way of giving whites fewer advantages. Although not all members of the alt-right share exactly the same views—for instance, some are anti-Semitic, while others do not have a problem with white Jews—they all believe America would be a better country with less racial diversity. Some interpret Trump's 2016

Steve Bannon, who serves as chief strategist in the Trump White House as of 2017, was previously employed as the executive chair of the alt-right website Breitbart News.

campaign slogan, "Make America Great Again," as referring to a time in America's past when people of color were not given a voice and white people were able to do and say whatever they wanted without fear of criticism.

The alt-right did not revive racism in the United States; people of color have always experienced racism directed toward them and have fought against it for years. However, the alt-right has brought racism back into the eyes of the white public. Some who previously denied that racism still existed in the United States have begun to see that it is, indeed, still an important social problem. Others still prefer to pretend that the problem does not exist because they are uncomfortable with facing their privilege. Being born with privilege does not make someone a bad person, but it is important for white people to be able to recognize the privilege they have, use it to be an ally to people of color, and actively join the fight against racism.

CHAPTER 4

Combating Racism

Many white people like the idea of ending racism but are not sure what they can do to help. They often ask people of color what white people should do, but this puts an unfair burden on people of color. It is the job of white people to educate themselves by reading books and articles about how to check their privilege and become better allies. They can also take cues, or hints, from people of color: If someone mentions that a certain thing makes them angry or uncomfortable, the white person can make a mental note not to do it in the future. When mistakes happen, rather than becoming defensive or angry, white people should apologize and attempt to learn from the situation.

Teaching Children about Race

Some people feel that it is inappropriate to teach children about racism, but the truth is that behavior is learned from a young age. Parents are often a child's first teachers. Children's earliest ideas about the way society works, as well as the ways in which people relate to one another, begin within the family setting. Parents and other family members typically lay the foundation for children's later attitudes toward others. Because of this, a child's ideas about people of other races begin within the home.

Racism often begins with the ideas and attitudes some parents instill in their children. Parents are in a unique position to combat racism, and they must be vigilant about challenging racism whenever it appears so that children learn tolerance and respect for others. If parents ignore the issue of racism until the child is older, the child will likely pick up negative opinions from other children, the media, or comments overheard in adult conversation.

Experts agree that all parents should discuss race and acceptance of others with their children. However, a 2007 study

Teaching children about racism from a young age will help them be more respectful of others as they grow up.

published in the *Journal of Marriage and Family* revealed a startling statistic. Of the 17,000 families of kindergarten-age children in the study, 75 percent of white parents rarely, if ever, spoke about race with their children. The author of a similar study on racist attitudes, Birgitte Vittrup of the Children's Research Lab at the University of Texas, offered one reason why parents may not discuss race openly with their children: Many simply do not feel comfortable doing so. When some of the parents dropped out of the study Vittrup was conducting, they told her, "We don't want to have these conversations with our child. We don't want to point out skin color."[37]

Some people may feel that any discussion of race or other characteristics that make another person "different" may be impolite. Further, they may fear that discussing race with their children will only make things worse. In fact, for years, the commonly held notion was that children did not notice another person's race unless it was pointed out to them. However, recent research indicates that children clearly begin to distinguish skin colors and make judgments based on them even as early as the preschool years. One experiment conducted at the University of Texas by psychology professor Rebecca Bigler studied the question of when children begin to notice racial differences. The experiment involved children who were four to five years old and was conducted in three preschool classrooms. The children were divided into two groups and randomly given either a blue or red t-shirt. For three weeks, the children wore these t-shirts. The teachers never mentioned the different colors, nor did they ever separate the children based on shirt color. When playing, the students did not self-segregate by shirt color.

RESPECT IS KEY

"The best and only sure way to prevent racism and racial violence is by reaching children and giving them the knowledge and tools they need to understand and respect both difference and inclusion. We would be amazed at the amount of positive change possible in our and their lifetimes."–Yolanda Moses, professor and Associate Vice Chancellor for Diversity, Equity and Excellence at the University of California, Riverside

Quoted in "Understanding 'Whiteness' and Unlearning Racism," American Anthropological Association, June 18, 2009. www.aaanet.org/issues/press/Understanding-Whiteness-and-Unlearning-Racism.cfm.

Still, when Bigler later asked the children which group was better to belong to, nearly all of them chose their own color. They also said they believed they were smarter than members of the other group. Although children responded that some of the members of the other group were mean, they said that none of the members of their own group were mean. The children had a clear sense of superiority regarding the other group. "The Reds never showed hatred for Blues," said Bigler. "It was more like, 'Blues are fine, but not as good as us.'"[38] Bigler concluded that children will use readily apparent differences, including skin color, to put people into categories and make distinctions between themselves and others. These categories are often reinforced by society. A 2003 study found that "by age 7, black children rated jobs held by blacks as lower in status than jobs held by whites."[39] Rather than having to decide for themselves what categories to separate people into, children pick up on the categories that already divide society.

Rodney Southern, a writer and father of two, agreed that even young children notice race. He said it is important that discussions of race and tolerance "start at a very young age. Kids form ideals very early, and we cannot underestimate the social dangers of waiting."[40]

Fighting Racism at School

In addition to parents, teachers are key figures in shaping a child's attitudes toward others. Just as parents can help prevent racism through discussions of values and tolerance in the home, teachers can also help prevent racism in the classroom. There are many classroom activities in use every day that help raise student awareness of racism. These include traditional activities such as reading and responding to poems, short stories, and novels written by people of color that deal with race and racism around the world. However, teachers can also find other ways to make the curriculum less Eurocentric and focus on the contributions of people of color.

Students can fight racism in several ways. One method is standing up to people, including friends, who make racist

COMMUNITY MATTERS

"Overall, there's not a lot of evidence that, at least in the long term, kids get their prejudice from their parents. I would call it more of a community effect than a parental effect. The community fosters tolerance or prejudice."—Charles Stangor, professor of psychology at the University of Maryland

Quoted in Sonia Scherr, "It Takes a Village to Raise a Racist," AlterNet, February 9, 2010. www.alternet.org/media/145596/it_takes_a_village_to_raise_a_racist.

remarks. Even if no one of that race is around to hear and be offended, it is important for people to call out that kind of behavior when they encounter it so others understand that it is not acceptable. Making racist remarks in private is a sign that someone will not treat people of color with respect.

Students also can and should report incidents of racism to a trusted adult, especially if the person being racist is a teacher. If the school does not take these incidents seriously, students can contact the American Civil Liberties Union (ACLU), an organization dedicated to standing up for the rights of Americans.

White students who are not directly affected by racism can be allies for people of color. Some ways to be a good ally include:

- Talk to other white people about racism and how it affects people of color.
- Confront racism when you see it happening.
- Apologize if you offend someone, and resist the urge to explain why you said what you did. People can still be offended even if no offense was meant.
- Make an effort to notice your privilege in everyday life.
- Be critical of news stories and the way they portray people of color versus white people.
- Listen to the stories people of color tell and make an effort to understand their point of view, but do not compare their struggle to your own life.
- Understand that you do not have to be included in everything just because you are white and that organizations specifically for people of color are not racist.
- Learn more about microaggressions and how to avoid them.
- Read books and articles written by people of color.

- Ask a parent or guardian for permission to attend a protest about a cause that affects people of color. Research the cause beforehand to understand what you are protesting.
- Do not expect to be praised or thanked for your actions. Do something because it is the right thing to do, not because you want to portray a certain image of yourself.

Wearing a safety pin has been suggested as a way for white people to show their support for people of color, but gestures such as this have been criticizedby some as providing a way for white people to make themselves feel better about racism without actually doing anything to fight it.

Challenging Racism in Society

Beyond the home and the classroom, racism can also be prevented in the community at large through programs that encourage racial tolerance. People around the world work to improve race relations through discussion groups, community education programs, and other activities. Founded in 1993, Seeds of Peace is an organization that offers programs around the world to help prevent racism by fostering the development of empathy and respect for others. One program is a yearly summer camp in Maine for young people of all races. There, the participants work on a series of team-building activities with the goal of bringing them in close contact with one another to develop mutual respect and empathy.

HEARING DIFFERENT VIEWS

"Exposure at an early age to a divergence of views plays a crucial part in laying the foundations for tolerance and understanding."–Tony Blair, former prime minister of the United Kingdom

Quoted in "Testimonials," Seeds of Peace. www.seedsofpeace.org/media/testimonials.

Another organization is the People's Institute for Survival and Beyond. Founded in 1980, the institute trains people to become effective community organizers. More than 100,000 people have gone through the institute's Undoing Racism Community Organizing Workshop, where they learn the basic skills necessary to lead anti-racist activities in their own communities, including effective community organizing, leadership development, coalition building, fundraising, and publicity.

The People's Institute also conducts a program called Youth Agenda. This program mentors young people in universities and throughout the communities in which the institute is active, helping them learn to recognize and speak out against racism in their own schools and communities.

Fighting Against the Dakota Access Pipeline

In 2016, members of the Standing Rock Sioux Tribe began protesting the Dakota Access Pipeline (DAPL), a pipeline to transport oil from North Dakota to Illinois. Many people were concerned that if the pipeline ever broke, it would poison the Sioux's water supply. Additionally, the Standing Rock Sioux submitted evidence to a court showing that the pipeline would destroy places that are sacred to the tribe. According to *The Atlantic*, "less than 24 hours after evidence of the new sacred sites were provided to the court, the Dakota Access company began construction on those same exact sites, perhaps destroying many of them forever."[1] This was a violation of regulations; the company should have waited for the court to decide whether or not it could go ahead with construction in light of the new evidence. By law, it also should have consulted with the Sioux about whether there were any sacred sites in the way of the pipeline.

Even though the Dakota Access company broke several laws, it was not punished, and the company still pushed for the pipeline to be constructed. The protest was originally not covered by any major news outlets but gained public support after being shared extensively on social media. In response to public support, President Obama halted construction. However, as one of his first acts as president, Trump allowed plans for construction to begin again, a decision that was quickly met with a new round of protests. The story of the DAPL shows that the U.S. government and private companies are still violating Native Americans' rights and breaking promises to them.

1. Robinson Meyer, "The Legal Case for Blocking the Dakota Access Pipeline," *The Atlantic*, September 9, 2016. www.theatlantic.com/technology/archive/2016/09/dapl-dakota-sitting-rock-sioux/499178/.

Even in 2017, Native Americans must fight to have their rights respected.

A number of other nonprofit organizations across the United States and around the world attempt to combat ongoing racism through education. One is A World of Difference Institute, sponsored by the Anti-Defamation League. Founded in Boston, Massachusetts, in 1985, A World of Difference provides diversity training to businesses as well as schools, universities, and communities. Through individual training programs, videos, discussion groups, and role-playing, A World of Difference Institute helps participants recognize bias, explore diversity, and improve relations between people of different races.

According to one Drexel University student, "each interactive workshop asked students to think critically about their own assumptions [and] … they discussed ways that students and faculty could be part of the solution to campus problems."[41]

Although community programs such as those offered by Seeds of Peace, the People's Institute for Survival and Beyond, and A World of Difference cannot completely end all racism, they can begin an important process. Dialogue between people of different backgrounds can lead to a greater awareness of racism and how to take steps to prevent it in the community.

Promoting Equality in the Workplace

Another arena in which there have been efforts to prevent racism is the workplace. In 2007, the EEOC introduced a nationwide initiative to combat racism. Known as E-RACE—Eradicating Racism and Colorism from Employment—the outreach program helps identify issues that often lead to discrimination and looks at strategies that may work in combating racism in businesses all across the United States. Most importantly, E-RACE tries to bring greater public awareness to the issues of race and color discrimination. By studying race in the workplace, E-RACE organizers hope to use technology to get a better idea about how common workplace prejudice is and how individual communities might work to eliminate it. According to William Tamayo, the district director of the EEOC's San Francisco, California, office, "the E-RACE Initiative urges us to understand and address the multifaceted and complex nature of racism in the 21st century so that

Colorblindness Is Not the Goal

In the past, many people would state that they were not racist because they were figuratively "colorblind," a term they used to mean that they did not notice the color of someone's skin. They said this to show that they were not basing their treatment of anyone on skin color and that they saw everyone as equals. However, many people, particularly people of color, have criticized this view. Because race is an important part of many people's identity, pretending not to notice it can be offensive, and people who bring it up may be accused of focusing too much on race. This can make it difficult for people of color to discuss their experiences with racism.

Pretending that race does not exist and is not an issue means that people who claim to be colorblind will often dismiss the idea that any unfair situation is the result of racism. Talking about race is sometimes uncomfortable, but it is impossible to solve a problem by pretending it does not exist. Rather than aiming for colorblindness, white people should focus on being good allies to people of color.

discrimination doesn't rob our nation of the contributions that a diverse population can make."[42]

Combating racism often means that a determined effort must be made to seek diversity when hiring employees. "Most companies have realized that mathematically, they cannot have the best talent available if minorities aren't represented,"[43] said Luke Visconti, the founder and chief executive officer of Diversity Inc., a diversity management consulting company.

However, Skidmore College history professor Jennifer Delton said the quest to hire a diverse workforce can be complex and confusing. Society, she explained, sends us conflicting messages about race and its importance in the workplace and in culture at large. "Diversity experts ask us to hold all of these competing views in our heads at once," she says. "Race matters. Race doesn't matter. It's fluid and invisible, but can also be classified and seen … It is a precarious foundation for fair, effective hiring policies."[44]

Scott E. Page, a professor at the University of Michigan, has spent years researching diversity in the workplace, and he is convinced that an organization's strength lies in its diversity. For Page, productivity, not prejudice, is the focus. "New York City is the perfect example of diversity functioning well," he said in an interview. "It's an exciting place that produces lots of innovation and creativity. It's not a coincidence that New York has so much energy and also so much diversity."[45] Using statistical models, Page determined that a variety of backgrounds working together often produces the best results for a company.

"People from different backgrounds have varying ways of looking at problems, what I call 'tools,'" Page said. "The sum of these tools is far more powerful in organizations with diversity than in ones where everyone has gone to the same schools, been trained in the same mold and thinks in almost identical ways."[46]

These efforts to prevent racism in the home, in schools, in the workplace, and in the community will determine how strong of a hold racism will continue to have on society. It may never be completely erased, but it may one day be possible to reduce its influence.

The Fight Continues

Racism is deeply ingrained in society, and the fight to dismantle it will be long and difficult. It will require people changing their attitudes and actions, which is hard when people are unaware of their biases and impossible when people do not see a problem with their beliefs. White people who are committed to helping end racism must learn how to be good allies, listen more, and examine their privilege. Racism cannot be overcome when the group in power is afraid of losing the benefits it believes it deserves.

An Inaccurate Image

Misunderstandings between people of different races can undermine efforts to deal effectively with racism. A failure to understand a person of a different race can often deepen tensions. For instance, when many Americans think of a terrorist, they picture a brown-skinned person, even though many shootings and bombings have been carried out by white people. The fear that everyone with brown skin—including Arabs, Middle Easterners, and Southeast Asians—could potentially be a Muslim extremist terrorist has had several different implications. First, it has caused some people to fear those who identify as Muslim, even though the vast majority of Muslims condemn the actions of radical extremists. Second, it has made some people assume that anyone with brown skin is a Muslim, even though they come from many different backgrounds and practice a variety of religions.

For example, Sikhism is a religion that is mainly practiced in India. Sikhs believe in one god and promote equality for everyone. Many Americans are unfamiliar with Sikhism and have often confused Sikhs for Muslims. Sikh men, who generally wear turbans and long beards as part of their faith, are particular targets because many Americans associate these features with Middle Eastern terrorists. According to *The Atlantic*, a nonprofit group called the Sikh Coalition "found that two-thirds of Sikh students get bullied at school. Students reported being accused of hiding grenades or bombs under their head coverings … In a group of 180 students surveyed in Fresno, California, a third

Sikhs such as this man are often confused for Muslims, and both groups are at risk for racially motivated verbal and physical attacks.

said they were bullied because their peers thought they look like terrorists."[47]

This focus on people from South Asia or the Middle East as the image of a terrorist harms innocent people and does not take into account the fact that white people also sometimes commit acts of terrorism. In January 2017, for instance, a 27-year-old Canadian white man named Alexandre Bissonette opened fire on a mosque in Quebec, killing six people. He had Islamophobic views that influenced his decision to carry out his terrorist attack at a mosque.

Fear of a particular group makes it more difficult to fight racism because people tend not to have an interest in getting to know someone they are afraid of. Avoiding someone out of fear makes it impossible to overcome negative stereotypes. For this reason, people have been encouraging others to get to know real Muslims. A woman named Tara Miele interviewed several Muslims for a short YouTube video called "Meet a Muslim," and a college junior named Aysha Yaqoob held a "Meet a Muslim" event at her school, the University of Regina in Saskatchewan, Canada. Miele and Yaqoob hope to give people an opportunity to challenge and broaden their views of Muslims so there is less hatred directed at them and others who are perceived to be Muslim.

The Impact of the President

When President Barack Obama was elected, many people saw this as proof that racism was no longer an issue in the United States. They were hopeful that he would be able to create policies to help people of color, especially other black people, gain more equality. However, according to Melissa Harris-Lacewell, an associate professor of politics and African American studies at Princeton University in New Jersey, "the election of a black president has not changed the material realities of racial inequality. African-Americans are significantly more distressed than their white counterparts on every meaningful economic indicator: income, unemployment, wealth, education, home ownership and home foreclosures."[48]

Obama also faced racism directed at him. After his election in 2008, some people protested him and his administration with racist messages, such as telling him to go back to Kenya, even though he had never lived there. Throughout all eight years of his presidency, he faced accusations that he had not been born in the United States; if this had been proven true, he would have had to step down as president, since the president must be born in the country. Donald Trump was one of Obama's most vocal critics, demanding that Obama show the public his birth certificate to prove he was a natural-born citizen. Even after Obama produced proof that he had been born in Hawaii, Trump and others continued to attack him, claiming that his birth certificate was fake.

President Trump has also had protests directed at him, but it is not because of the color of his skin. Most of the protestors have called him racist, sexist, and xenophobic (afraid of foreigners) due to public statements he has made. After he signed an executive order restricting immigration to the United States from some Muslim-majority countries, protests sprang up around the country. Some people went to major airports to show their support for refugees and immigrants. This executive order has been referred to as a "Muslim ban" by opponents because it affected people from countries where Islam is the main religion. Trump's supporters pointed out that his executive order never mentioned the word "Muslim" and said the ban was necessary to prevent terrorists from posing as immigrants and coming into the country. However, although the order did not specifically mention the word "Muslim," it did say that after the ban is lifted, the Department of Homeland Security will "prioritize refugee claims made by individuals on the basis of religious-based persecution, provided that the religion of the individual is a minority religion in the individual's country of nationality."[49] Since Islam is the majority religion in the affected countries, the order means that non-Muslims will be given preference.

Thousands of people around the world protested the American travel ban.

Disney and Diversity

Ever since Snow White first fell in love with Prince Charming in 1937, the faces of Disney heroines have been almost uniformly white. Then in 1992, the film studio released *Aladdin*, which featured Jasmine as the first non-white Disney princess. In 1995, it released *Pocahontas*, based on the real Pocahontas, a Native American woman. Three years later, Disney released *Mulan*, the story of a girl who disguises herself as a boy so she can join the Chinese army, and in 2002, the studio released *Lilo & Stitch*, a movie about a Hawaiian girl (Lilo) and her pet alien (Stitch). In 2009, *The Princess and the Frog* featured Tiana, a young black girl who dreams of owning a restaurant, and in 2016, *Moana* told the story of a Polynesian girl trying to save her home.

Disney has been criticized for some of these movies and praised for others. *Pocahontas*, for instance, ends in a way that implies the settlers and Native Americans will become friends, although this is not historically accurate. *The Princess and the Frog* was criticized for showing negative stereotypes of black people. *Moana* also faced accusations of stereotyping Polynesians but was praised because the actors who voiced the characters were people of color. Many people hope that Disney will continue its trend of diversity in the future, but with even more sensitivity.

The executive order was criticized for several reasons. First, although the executive order talked about the terrorist attacks of September 11, 2001, the countries where those terrorists came from were not included in the ban. Some have accused Trump of leaving them out because he has business dealings there, but the White House denied this, stating that the countries were chosen based on a list made by the Obama administration.

Second, the ban affected people with visas and green cards—people who had already been approved to live and work in the

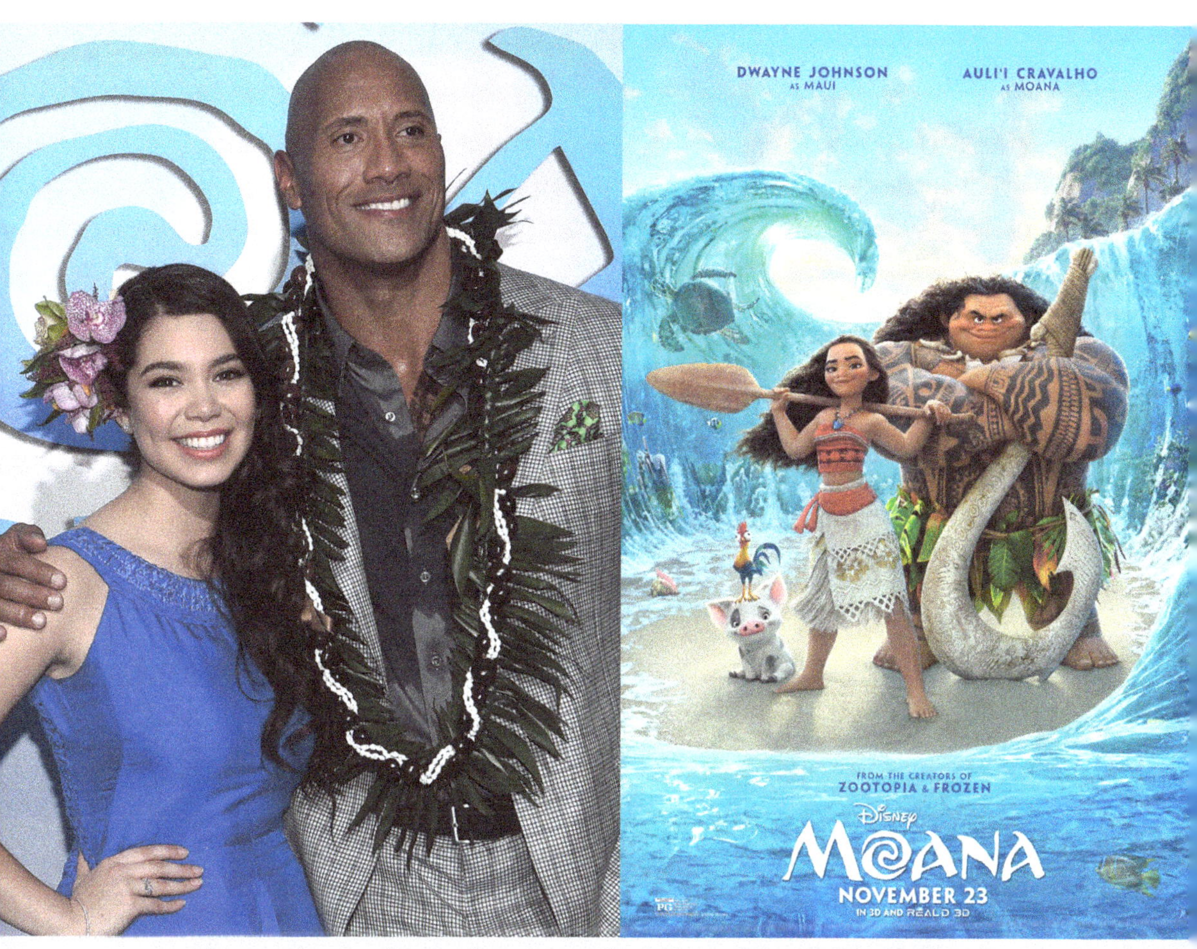

Many people praised Disney for using people of color, including Auli'i Cravalho and Dwayne "The Rock" Johnson, to voice the characters in Moana.

United States. Some people with green cards who were out of the country when the ban went into effect had difficulty getting back in and had to go through extra security screenings, although the Department of Homeland Security promised that no one would be denied entry if the extra screenings did not reveal a history of terrorism.

Third, the ban has been widely criticized as racist because it implies that everyone from the countries on the list is a potential threat. According to CNN, "9 people have been killed a year, on average, by Muslim extremists in the US since 9/11." In contrast, "12,843 people are killed a year, on average, by guns in the US."[50] Although terrorism is a serious issue, many people believe that rather than making Americans safer, the only effect a ban will have is to harm people who are fleeing war and terrorism in their own countries, particularly Syria.

As of early 2017, the courts have halted the Trump administration's travel bans on more than one occasion. However, court rulings can be appealed, so the idea of a ban is unlikely to go away any time soon.

Less Emphasis on Skin Color

Anthropologist Nina Jablonski imagined a future in which color remains a fact of life, but fewer distinctions based on color exist. She said 1,000 years from now, people "will still come in lots of colors, but in big cities, where many people from different places live and mix, there will be even more who have 'in-between' skin colors and fewer people with strikingly dark or light complexions."[51]

Complexion, or skin tone, is already a complicated subject. People who identify themselves as white may have genetically darker skin than many white people, whereas self-identifying black people may appear lighter than some white people. Scholar Henry Louis Gates Jr. said "race" is a relative term. All people, he suggested, are of mixed race, products of a complicated history. Tests of deoxyribonucleic acid (DNA)—the carrier of people's genetic information—that can determine the exact percentage of a person's racial makeup, he said, will prove this fact in the years to come. "The more we use DNA tests to trace our family trees, the more we're going to discover just how tangled our roots really are," Gates said. "We are all mulattoes [biracial people] of one kind or another. In the end, what actually makes us black or white? Or have those terms become outdated?"[52]

The answer to Gates's question may lie within the recent work of geneticists. Scientists have mapped the human genome, the complex code of human life, and determined that all human beings are genetically the same. Race, therefore, is simply a social construction with no basis in science. Any differences between races are likely a result of historical developments, such as wars, slavery, migration patterns, and agriculture. In tracing human history to its roots, scientists have concluded that all human beings originated on the African continent some 200,000 years ago. Thus, a common ancestor may connect all of humanity. According to biological anthropologist Alan Goodman, "all skin colors, whether light or dark, are not due to race but to adaptation for life under the sun."[53] Over thousands of years, people developed the best skin color to suit their environment. People in warmer climates, such as Africa and India, have darker skin because it protects them from sunburn; people in colder climates, such as Norway, have lighter skin because it helps them absorb enough sunlight to produce vitamin D. These traits developed over millions of years and are passed on genetically, so even if someone moves from one type of climate to another, their skin color will not change dramatically.

Despite the scientific proof that racial differences are genetically meaningless, some people remain convinced that races are categories that can be used to understand human behavior,

Darker skin acts as natural protection from the sun.

morality, or intelligence. In the United States and other countries around the world, defining people by the color of their skin is a kind of shorthand by which people are viewed and often judged, for better and for worse. "You are what you have to defend," said actor Don Cheadle. "Cause it doesn't matter that I'm 19% European and 81% African. In America, I have to deal with the problems that black people in America have."[54]

Integration in Schools

American schools legally separated black students from white ones until the 1954 *Brown v. Board of Education* Supreme Court decision made the practice illegal. However, some schools remain segregated today because school officials "do not know the status of their desegregation orders, have never read them, or erroneously [wrongly] believe that orders have been ended."[55] Some people do not believe segregation is a problem, but research has shown that "desegregated schools are linked to important benefits, like prejudice reduction, heightened civic engagement and analytical thinking, and better learning outcomes in general."[56] Students who have a chance to interact with people who are different than them will learn more and become better informed about racial and cultural issues. Additionally, according to *The Atlantic*, "most African American and Hispanic students attend public schools where a majority of their classmates qualify as poor or low-income."[57] This affects the schools and the quality of the children's education for a number of reasons: "They are in poorer communities, they have less local resources, they have fewer parents with college degrees, they have fewer two parent families where there are parents who can come spend time volunteering in the school, they have a harder time attracting the best teachers."[58]

Rita Jones Turner does not agree that forced integration is no longer necessary. In 1970, she became one of the first black students to attend Vestavia Hills High School in Birmingham, Alabama, after forced desegregation. She remembered that the school bus often would not stop on her street. At school, she was placed into remedial classes even

Genetic Tests Are Unreliable

Some companies, including Ancestry DNA, 23andMe, and Family Tree DNA, offer genetic tests to help people discover their ancestry. Sometimes people are surprised by the results; for instance, when Pearl Duncan, a black woman, took the test, it told her she was 10 percent Scottish. DNA tests are relatively expensive, but for people who are willing to pay, the test can be a fun experiment.

However, experts caution against taking DNA tests as proof of ancestry. Since race is a socially created idea, there is no gene that determines it. *Slate* magazine explained,

Our genes dictate certain things about us–there's a gene that programs the color of your eyes, for example. But ethnicity is not a trait derived from a single gene, because ethnicity is mostly our perception of a collection of traits, rather than a trait itself. So a genetic test that looks at our genes and comes back with an assessment of our ethnic roots isn't honing in on a specific gene and reading what it says because there's no such gene to read. Instead, the test is comparing snippets of our DNA to snippets of DNA of people of known origin and looking for similarities.

The problem is that DNA snippets, or markers, are inconsistent. Sometimes they are passed on and sometimes they are not, and whether they are or aren't is random … So when a DNA test comes back saying you are 28 percent Finnish, all it's really saying is that of the DNA analyzed … 28 percent of it was most similar to that of a completely Finnish person. In the end, these comparisons are a fun but ultimately unreliable way to think about the possibilities of [who] your ancestors might have been, rather than definitive proof of your ethnic background.[1]

1. Matt Miller, "A DNA Test Won't Explain Elizabeth Warren's Ancestry," *Slate*, June 29, 2016. www.slate.com/articles/technology/future_tense/2016/06/dna_testing_cannot_determine_ancestry_including_elizabeth_warren_s.html.

though she did not need extra help, and at lunchtime, white students harassed her by tearing barrettes from her hair.

Thirty-six years later, Jones Turner received a note from her old school informing her of its attempt to change the policy of desegregation and force her ninth-grade son to enroll elsewhere.

Studies have shown that desegregated schools have many benefits for students and the community.

Specifically, the school district filed a court motion to stop forced integration. Jones Turner's own experience at Vestavia Hills remained a painful memory, but she resented any attempts at turning back the clock on progress. "We were used, mistreated, downtrodden, and discriminated against," Jones Turner said. "I have no problem with being a sacrificial lamb for the good of the community, but to have the system back out now is not fair. They made a commitment to educate black children."[59]

The Vestavia Hills school board denied any racial motivation in wanting to halt integration; instead, the board claimed that economics forced their decision. The school said its budget could no longer bear the strain of busing black students from all the way across town. A judge ruled in favor of the school.

DIFFERING VIEWS OF LANGUAGE

"[People] will read a book that's one third Elvish, but put two sentences in Spanish and they [white people] think we're taking over."—Junot Díaz, author

Quoted in Erin Cossetta, "23 Quotes That Perfectly Explain Racism (To People Who Don't 'See Color')," *Thought Catalog*, May 1, 2014. thoughtcatalog.com/erin-cossetta/2014/04/quotes-that-perfectly-explain-racism-to-people-who-dont-see-color/.

School segregation affects more than just schools. According to writer Roger Shuler, "The euphemism you hear in the Birmingham real-estate game is that cities such as Mountain Brook, Vestavia Hills, and Homewood have 'good schools.' That means they have overwhelmingly white schools, and many home buyers are willing to pay hugely inflated prices to live in those areas."[60] The rising cost of housing means many families of color cannot afford to live in those areas, so they cannot send their children to those schools.

Race and the Future

After Obama's first election in 2008, *Forbes* published an article declaring, "Racism in America Is Over."[61] However, as police brutality against black people became more commonly reported, it was clear to some people that racism was still an issue in the United States, although others still denied it. After Trump's election in 2016, some white people expressed shock; they assumed he would lose the election because many perceived him to be racist, sexist, and xenophobic. However, according to the *New York Times*, "when [Tunette Powell, a black Ph.D. student in Los Angeles] and other black Americans were interviewed recently about Mr. Trump's candidacy, shock was rarely a word that came to mind. More often, they said, what they felt was a numbing familiarity: What the rest of America was now being exposed to are words and thoughts they have heard their whole lives."[62]

SILENCE IS A CHOICE

"If you are neutral in situations of injustice, you have chosen the side of the oppressor. If an elephant has its foot on the tail of a mouse, and you say that you are neutral, the mouse will not appreciate your neutrality."–Desmond Tutu, retired Anglican archbishop and South African social rights activist

Quoted in Erin Cossetta, "23 Quotes That Perfectly Explain Racism (To People Who Don't 'See Color')," *Thought Catalog*, May 1, 2014. thoughtcatalog.com/erin-cossetta/2014/04/quotes-that-perfectly-explain-racism-to-people-who-dont-see-color/.

Although racism against black people has been prominent in the news, especially after the creation of the BLM movement, other groups who experience racism are rarely talked about. Data from the Centers for Disease Control and Prevention (CDC) that was "collected from medical examiners in 47 states between 1999 and 2011" found that "[w]hen compared to their percentage of the U.S. population, Natives were more likely to be killed by police than any other group, including African Americans."[63] However, the U.S. media rarely reports these killings. Although BLM has received much media attention, a similar initiative called Native Lives Matter, started in 2014, has gone almost entirely unreported. According to

Many white Americans are interested in Native American culture but do not want to hear about the racism Native Americans face.

Lydia Millet, a writer for the *New York Times*, "When it comes to American Indians, mainstream America suffers from willful blindness."[64] Some would rather not hear about issues such as these because it makes them feel sad, frustrated, or defensive. However, ignoring problems does not make them disappear.

Racism against Asians is also rarely spoken about, and because the mainstream perception of Asians is generally positive, many people deny that it exists. However, racial slurs and microaggressions are commonly directed at people in this racial group, and they are largely ignored in the media. This lack of attention to Asians and any problems they may be facing is itself a form of racism.

Bias based on race has not faded, but it has been complicated by the addition of bias based on religion, especially a religion practiced mainly by people of a certain race. Muslims and people who are mistaken for Muslims have been the target of hate crimes for years, but the intensity of people's fear and hatred for these groups has increased in the last decade. Fears about non-white immigrants have also enhanced racism toward Latinx that has existed for many years.

SOCIETY MUST CHANGE

"I don't think what's in people's heads is going to change until the environment that places these things in their head has changed."
–Anthony Greenwald, professor of psychology at the University of Washington

Quoted in Elizabeth Landau, "You May Be More Racist than You Think, Study Says," CNN, April 2, 2009. edition.cnn.com/2009/HEALTH/01/07/racism.study/index.html.

For victims of racial or religious prejudice alike, justice will never be entirely possible without a commitment to creating laws that protect people from discrimination. Although no law can legislate attitudes and fears, there is hope that the struggle for racial progress will continue well into the

21st century and beyond. To create change, people must be willing to continue fighting, and white people in particular must be committed to challenging their privileged roles in society.

NOTES

Introduction: Racism Is Not New

1. "Institutional Racism," Racism. No way!, 2015. www.racismnoway.com.au/teaching-resources/factsheets/32.html.

2. Robert Chrisman and Ernest Allen Jr., "Ten Reasons: A Response to David Horowitz," University of Massachusetts Amherst. www.umass.edu/afroam/hor.html.

Chapter 1: Modern-Day Racism

3. Quoted in Beverly Daniel Tatum, *"Why Are All the Black Kids Sitting Together in the Cafeteria?": And Other Conversations About Race*. New York, NY: Basic Books, 1999, p. 7.

4. Niall McCarthy, "Report: Trump's Election Led to a Surge in Hate Crimes [Infographic]," *Forbes*, November 30, 2016. www.forbes.com/sites/niallmccarthy/2016/11/30/report-trumps-election-led-to-a-surge-in-hate-crime-infographic/#4d74a1125f0d.

5. Quoted in Katya Adler, "Spain Reflects on Football Racism Row," BBC News, November 18, 2004. news.bbc.co.uk/2/hi/europe/4024167.stm.

6. Quoted in Adler, "Spain Reflects on Football Racism Row."

7. Quoted in Adler, "Spain Reflects on Football Racism Row."

8. Quoted in Rachel Donadio, "Race Riots Grip Italian Town, and Mafia Is Suspected," *New York Times*, January 10, 2010. www.nytimes.com/2010/01/11/world/europe/11italy.html?emc=eta1.

9. Quoted in Dan Gilgoff, "Investing in Diversity," *U.S. News & World Report*, November 1, 2009, p. 72.

10. Clarence Otis Jr., interview by Ed Gordon, *News and Notes*, National Public Radio, April 11, 2006. www.npr.org/templates/story/story.php?storyId=5336052.

11. Quoted in Annette Walker, "Black and Latino Workers Win $21 Million Discrimination Lawsuit Against Parks Dept.," *New Amsterdam News*, April 17–23, 2008.

12. Quoted in Heben Nigatu, "21 Racial Microaggressions You Hear on a Daily Basis," BuzzFeed, December 9, 2013. www.buzzfeed.com/hnigatu/racial-microagressions-you-hear-on-a-daily-basis?utm_term=.pa3oQ0m9Y#.keNavP2XK.

13. Quoted in Elizabeth Landau, "You May Be More Racist than You Think, Study Says," CNN.com, April 2, 2009. edition.cnn.com/2009/HEALTH/01/07/racism.study.

14. Molefi Kete Asante, *Erasing Racism: The Survival of the African Nation*. Amherst, NY: Prometheus, 2003, p. 254.

15. Sharon H. Chang, "Opinion: Closure of POC Yoga Due to Hate, Death Threats a Tragedy for All People of Color," *International Examiner*, October 18, 2015. www.iexaminer.org/2015/10/poc-yoga-closure-a-tragedy.

Chapter 2: Factors of Racism

16. Tatum, *"Why Are All the Black Kids Sitting Together in the Cafeteria?,"* pp. 3–4.

17. "Racism and Psychology," American Psychological Association. www.apa.org/pi/oema/resources/brochures/racism.aspx.

18. Stephen Lloyd, "Queer Eyes, Full Hearts," *Modern Family*, season 6, episode 7, directed by Jason Winer, aired

September 12, 2014.

19. American Psychological Association, "Racism and Psychology."

20. "Maryland Police Question U.S. Citizen's Immigration Status," CBS News, January 28, 2017. www.cbsnews.com/news/maryland-police-question-us-citizen-immigration-status.

21. Camila Domonoske and Bill Chappell, "Minnesota Gov. Calls Traffic Stop Shooting 'Absolutely Appalling at All Levels,'" NPR, July 7, 2016. www.npr.org/sections/thetwo-way/2016/07/07/485066807/police-stop-ends-in-black-mans-death-aftermath-is-livestreamed-online-video.

22. Rob Wile, "Watch DeRay Mckesson Give the Perfect Response to a CNN Anchor's Question About 'All Lives Matter,'" *Fusion*, July 18, 2016. fusion.net/story/326453/deray-mckesson-cnn-all-lives-matter-black-lives-matter.

23. Malcolm Gladwell, *Blink*. New York, NY: Little, Brown, 2005, p. 143.

24. "Poverty in the United States: Frequently Asked Questions," National Poverty Center. www.npc.umich.edu/poverty/.

25. "Poverty in the United States: Frequently Asked Questions," National Poverty Center.

26. Shawn Regan, "5 Ways the Government Keeps Native Americans in Poverty," *Forbes*, March 13, 2014. www.forbes.com/sites/realspin/2014/03/13/5-ways-the-government-keeps-native-americans-in-poverty/#57d5dc466cc6.

27. Jens Manuel Krogstad, "One-in-four Native Americans and Alaska Natives Are Living in Poverty," Pew Research Center, June 13, 2014. www.pewresearch.org/

fact-tank/2014/06/13/1-in-4-native-americans-and-alaska-natives-are-living-in-poverty.

28. Huizhong Wu, "The 'Model Minority' Myth: Why Asian-American Poverty Goes Unseen," Mashable, December 14, 2015. mashable.com/2015/12/14/asian-american-poverty/#bPeJ311FEgqO.

Chapter 3: Racism in Society

29. Nadra Kareem Nittle, "What Is Cultural Appropriation and Why Is it Wrong?," About News, November 14, 2016. racerelations.about.com/od/diversitymatters/fl/What-Is-Cultural-Appropriation-and-Why-Is-It-Wrong.htm.

30. Adrienne K., "But Why Can't I Wear a Hipster Headdress?" Native Appropriations, April 27, 2010. nativeappropriations.com/2010/04/but-why-cant-i-wear-a-hipster-headdress.html.

31. Anjali Joshi, "Why a Bindi is NOT an Example of Cultural Appropriation," *Huffington Post*, April 15, 2014. www.huffingtonpost.com/anjali-joshi/why-a-bindi-is-not-an-exa_b_5150693.html.

32. Lyndon B. Johnson, "To Fulfill These Rights," commencement address, Howard University, Washington, DC, June 4, 1965. online.hillsdale.edu/document.doc?id=286.

33. Quoted in Linda Greenhouse, *Becoming Justice Blackmun: Harry Blackmun's Supreme Court Journey*. New York, NY: Times Books, 2005, p. 133.

34. Ross Douthat, "Race in 2028," *New York Times*, July 19, 2009. www.nytimes.com/2009/07/20/opinion/20douthat.html.

35. Quoted in Joseph Williams and Matt Negrin, "Affirmative Action Foes Point to Obama," *Boston Globe*,

March 18, 2008. www.boston.com/news/nation/articles/2008/03/18/affirmative_action_foes_point_to_obama.

36. John Blake, "This Is What 'Whitelash' Looks Like," CNN, November 19, 2016. www.cnn.com/2016/11/11/us/obama-trump-white-backlash.

Chapter 4: Combating Racism

37. Quoted in Po Bronson and Ashley Merryman, "See Baby Discriminate," *Newsweek*, September 14, 2009. www.newsweek.com/id/214989/page/1.

38. Quoted in Bronson and Merryman, "See Baby Discriminate."

39. Melinda Wenner Moyer, "Teaching Tolerance," *Slate*, March 30, 2014. www.slate.com/articles/double_x/the_kids/2014/03/teaching_tolerance_how_white_parents_should_talk_to_their_kids_about_race.html.

40. Rodney Southern, "How to Prevent Racism in Your Child," Associated Content, October 17, 2007. www.associatedcontent.com/article/407029/how_to_prevent_racism_in_your_ child.html?cat=25.

41. Quoted in Anti-Defamation League, "A World of Difference Institute: A Campus of Difference." www.adl.org/education/edu_awod/awod_campus.asp.

42. Quoted in "EEOC Takes a New Approach to Fighting Racism and Colorism in the 21st Century Workplace," U.S. Equal Employment Opportunity Commission, February 28, 2007. www.eeoc.gov/eeoc/newsroom/re lease/2-28-07.cfm.

43. Quoted in Gilgoff, "Investing in Diversity," p. 73.

44. Jennifer Delton, "Why Diversity for Diversity's Sake Won't Work," *Chronicle of Higher Education*, September 28, 2007, pp. B32–B33.

45. Quoted in Claudia Dreifus, "In Professor's Model, Diversity = Productivity," *New York Times*, January 8, 2008. www.nytimes.com/2008/01/08/science/08conv.html.

46. Quoted in Dreifus, "In Professor's Model, Diversity = Productivity."

Chapter 5: The Fight Continues

47. Emma Green, "The Trouble with Wearing Turbans in America," *The Atlantic*, January 27, 2015. www.theatlantic.com/politics/archive/2015/01/the-trouble-with-wearing-turbans-in-america/384832.

48. Melissa Harris-Lacewell, "Commentary: Racial Progress Is Far from Finished," CNN, June 5, 2009. edition.cnn.com/2009/LIVING/07/07/lacewell.post.racial/index.html.

49. "Executive Order: Protecting the Nation from Foreign Terrorist Entry into the United States," the White House, January 27, 2017. www.whitehouse.gov/the-press-office/2017/01/27/executive-order-protecting-nation-foreign-terrorist-entry-united-states.

50. AJ Willingham, Paul Martucci, and Natalie Leung, "The Chances of a Refugee Killing You—and Other Suprising Immigration Stats," CNN, January 31, 2017. www.cnn.com/2017/01/30/politics/immigration-stats-by-the-numbers-trnd.

51. Quoted in American Anthropological Association, "Only Skin Deep," RACE Project. www.understandingrace.com/humvar/skin_03.html.

52. Quoted in Ashlinn Quinn, "Rationalizing Race in U.S. History," *African American Lives 2*, PBS. www.pbs.org/wnet/aalives/teachers/rationalizing_race.html.

53. Quoted in American Anthropological Association, "Only Skin Deep."

54. Quoted in Quinn, "Rationalizing Race in U.S. History."

55. Nikole Hannah-Jones, "School Districts Still Face Fights—and Confusion—on Integration," *The Atlantic*, May 2, 2014. www.theatlantic.com/education/archive/2014/05/lack-of-order-the-erosion-of-a-once-great-force-for-integration/361563.

56. Lauren Camera, "The New Segregation," *U.S. News & World Report*, July 26, 2016. www.usnews.com/news/articles/2016-07-26/racial-tensions-flare-as-schools-resegregate.

57. Janie Boschma and Ronald Brownstein, "The Concentration of Poverty in American Schools," *The Atlantic*, February 29, 2016. www.theatlantic.com/education/archive/2016/02/concentration-poverty-american-schools/471414/

58. Quoted in Boschma and Brownstein, "The Concentration of Poverty in American Schools."

59. Quoted in Jenny Jarvie, "School Seeks to End Racial Integration," *Boston Globe*, October 29, 2006. www.boston.com/news/education/k_12/articles/2006/10/29/school_seeks_to_end_racial_integration.

60. Roger Shuler, "School Segregation Is Taking New Forms," *Daily Kos*, January 29, 2010. www.dailykos.com/story/2010/1/29/831859/-.

61. John McWhorter, "Racism in America Is Over," *Forbes*, December 30, 2008. www.forbes.com/2008/12/30/end-of-racism-oped-cx_jm_1230mcwhorter.html.

62. Yamiche Alcindor, "Black Voters on Donald Trump: We've Heard It All Before," *New York Times*, October 25, 2016. www.nytimes.com/2016/10/26/us/politics/donald-trump-black-voters.html.

63. Stephanie Woodard, "The Police Killings No One Is Talking About," *In These Times*, October 17, 2016. inthesetimes.com/features/native_american_police_killings_native_lives_matter.html.

64. Lydia Millet, "Native Lives Matter, Too," *New York Times*, October 13, 2015. www.nytimes.com/2015/10/13/opinion/native-lives-matter-too.html.

DISCUSSION QUESTIONS

Chapter 1: Modern-Day Racism

1. Have you experienced racism in your own life?
2. Describe some microaggressions different groups might encounter, and discuss how they can be avoided.
3. Why is "reverse racism" a myth?
4. Discuss examples of intersectionality.

Chapter 2: Factors of Racism

1. What are some of the ways in which stereotypes can be harmful to people?
2. Why is race a meaningless concept?
3. How does racial profiling contribute to racism?
4. What biases do you hold? How can you overcome them?

Chapter 3: Racism in Society

1. In your opinion, is affirmative action helpful or harmful?
2. Give examples of cultural appropriation and why they are wrong.
3. Why is whitewashing problematic?
4. Why has the alt-right been compared to the Nazi Party?

Chapter 4: Combating Racism

1. What are some ways you can fight racism?
2. How can white people become better allies to people of color?
3. Why is it problematic for people to say they are "colorblind" when it comes to race?
4. How does diversity benefits schools and companies?

Chapter 5: The Fight Continues

1. How are Islamophobia and racism similar? How are they different?
2. Why have President Trump's immigration restrictions been called a "Muslim ban"?
3. Why is segregation in schools a problem?
4. Do you think racism can ever be completely eliminated? Why or why not?

ORGANIZATIONS TO CONTACT

American Civil Liberties Union (ACLU)
125 Broad Street
18th Floor
New York, NY 10004
(212) 549-2500
www.aclu.org
Founded in 1920, the ACLU protects the rights of Americans from overreach by schools, businesses, and the government.

Amnesty International (USA Headquarters)
5 Penn Plaza
16th Floor
New York, NY 10001
(212) 807-8400
www.amnestyusa.org
Amnesty International is a worldwide organization that campaigns for internationally recognized human rights for all. The organization's supporters work to end injustice and to improve human rights through campaigning and international solidarity. The U.S. chapter focuses on injustice specifically in the United States.

Human Rights Watch
350 Fifth Avenue
34th Floor
New York, NY 10118
(212) 290-4700
www.hrw.org
As one of the world's leading independent defenders and protectors of human rights, Human Rights Watch works to focus international attention where human rights are being violated.

National Association for the Advancement of Colored People (NAACP)
4805 Mt. Hope Drive
Baltimore, MD 21215
(877) NAACP-98
www.naacp.org
Founded in 1909, the NAACP has championed social justice and fought for the civil rights of black people for more than a century.

The People's Institute for Survival and Beyond
601 North Carrollton Avenue
New Orleans, LA 70119
(504) 301-9292
www.pisab.org
This national and international collective of antiracist, multicultural community organizers and educators is dedicated to building an effective movement for social transformation through its Undoing Racism and Community Organizing workshops. The institute helps individuals, communities, organizations, and institutions address the causes of racism to create a more fair and equal society.

Southern Poverty Law Center (SPLC)
400 Washington Avenue
Montgomery, AL 36104
(334) 956-8200
www.splcenter.org
Founded in 1971, the SPLC is internationally known for its tolerance education programs, its legal victories against white supremacists, and its tracking of hate groups. The SPLC fights all forms of discrimination and works to protect society's most vulnerable members. It has achieved significant legal victories, including landmark Supreme Court decisions, against hate groups.

FOR MORE INFORMATION

Books

Cruz, Bárbara. *The Fight for Latino Civil Rights*. New York, NY: Enslow Publishing, 2016.
Members of the Latinx community, like other people of color, have fought long and hard for their rights in the United States. This book describes the history of their struggle and the work that still must be done.

Leatherboy, Mary Beth, and Lisa Charleyboy. *Urban Tribes: Native Americans in the City*. Toronto, ON: Annick Press, 2015.
This book confronts stereotypes using works by young, urban Native Americans that explore how they relate to their cultures in the present day.

Marrin, Albert. *Uprooted: The Japanese American Experience During World War II*. New York, NY: Knopf Books for Young Readers, 2016.
After the Japanese bombed Pearl Harbor in World War II, Americans feared that any Japanese person might be a terrorist. Many American citizens of Japanese descent who had done nothing wrong were forced to leave their homes and enter prison camps, where they remained for much of the war. This horrible part of American history is echoed in the current mistrust of Muslim immigrants and described in this book.

Steele, Philip. *Race and Crime*. London, UK: Wayland, 2014.
Steele allows readers to learn about the ways race affects crime rates and incidents of police brutality.

Tatum, Beverly Daniel. *"Why Are All the Black Kids Sitting Together in the Cafeteria?": And Other Conversations About Race*.

New York, NY: Basic Books, 2003.
Psychologist Beverly Daniel Tatum discusses the ways racism still affects interactions between white people and people of color.

Websites

Let's Fight Racism!
www.un.org/en/letsfightracism
This website, a project of the United Nations, gives people the opportunity to learn more about different racial groups to decrease the fear and ignorance that lead to racism.

Project Implicit
implicit.harvard.edu/implicit/takeatest.html
Take an IAT to discover biases you may not know you have about race, gender, sexuality, age, and more.

RACE: Are We So Different?
www.understandingrace.com
Developed by the American Anthropological Association, this is the website of the RACE Project, which explains the differences among people and reveals the reality and unreality of race. The website includes a brief film on the evolution of race in America, an interactive timeline, and articles on the science of race.

Showing Up for Racial Justice
www.showingupforracialjustice.org
This campaign helps white people organize to show support for their local racial justice groups.

Teaching Tolerance
www.tolerance.org
This website is a project of the Southern Poverty Law Center. It features a wide range of resources that encourage understanding and acceptance among races.

INDEX

PICTURE CREDITS

Cover Michael B. Thomas/Getty Images; pp. 6–7 National Geographic Creative/Alamy Stock Photo; pp. 8–9 Joseph Sohm/Shutterstock.com; p. 19 michaeljung/Shutterstock.com; pp. 22–23 Jupiterimages/Stockbyte/ Getty Images; p. 27 WAYHOME studio/Shutterstock.com; p. 31 Ollyy/ Shutterstock.com; p. 34 Taraskin/Shutterstock.com; p. 35 Tinseltown/ Shutterstock.com; pp. 38–39 RichLegg/E+/Getty Images; p. 40 Ira Bostic/ Shutterstock.com; p. 42 Steve Collender/Shutterstock.com; p. 44 Spencer Platt/Getty Images; pp. 46–47 Carl Mydans/The LIFE Picture Collection/ Getty Images; p. 49 Markus Cuff/Corbis Documentary/Getty Images; p. 51 Pictorial Press Ltd/Alamy Stock Photo; pp. 54–55 Bruce Glikas/Bruce Glikas/FilmMagic/Getty Images; p. 56 Dima Sidelnikov/Shutterstock.com; p. 61 Win McNamee/Getty Images; p. 64 © istockphoto.com/FatCamera; p. 68 Maen Zayyad/Shutterstock.com; pp. 70–71 ROBYN BECK/AFP/ Getty Images; p. 76 ArtWell/Shutterstock.com; pp. 78–79 Zach Gibson/ Getty Images; p. 81 (left) Alberto E. Rodriguez/Getty Images for Disney; p. 81 (right) Collection Christophel/Alamy Stock Photo; p. 83 mimagephotography/Shutterstock.com; p. 86 Monkey Business Images/ Shutterstock.com; p. 89 Jane Rix/Shutterstock.com.

ABOUT THE AUTHOR

Meghan Green has edited a number of books for young people on the topics of social justice and self-esteem. She also sometimes gives talks at local schools on these topics. She is a social worker who specializes in working with developmentally disabled individuals. Meghan lives in Pennsylvania with her husband, Kris.